STRIVING FOR EXCELLENCE IN THE SOCIAL SECTOR

A Decade of Distinction

Eric Schmall
Center for Nonprofit Excellence
Louisville, Kentucky

CENTER FOR
NONPROFIT EXCELLENCE
Your Excellence is Our Passion

Copyright © 2010 by Center for Nonprofit Excellence.

All rights reserved. No part of this book may be reproduced in any form or by any electronic or mechanical means, including information storage and retrieval systems, without permission in writing from the publisher, except by a reviewer who may quote brief passages in a review.

Clark Legacies, LLC
520 Old Stone Lane
Louisville, KY 40207

Visit our Web site at www.ClarkLegacies.com

First Edition: September 2010

Printed in the United States of America.
10 9 8 7 6 5 4 3 2 1

ISBN: 978-0-9827453-7-3

DEDICATION

To all those who work in and support the goals of the social sector in the quest to improve our communities, this nation, and the world through their visionary resolve.

"... *to strive, to seek, to find, and not to yield.*"
— Alfred Lord Tennyson, "Ulysses"

ACKNOWLEDGEMENTS

This book developed out of an idea of memorializing the examples of excellence that have emerged in the Metro Louisville region's social sector during the first decade of the Center for Nonprofit Excellence's existence.

Special acknowledgements are certainly owed to the group that investigated the need for and ultimately designed the model of a resource center for social sector organizations that became The Center for Nonprofit Excellence (CNPE). We salute those early visionaries: Dale Tucker, Joe Tolan, Howard Mason, Scott Davis, Bruce Maza, Jim Davis, Barry Barker, Bob Adams, Eunice Blocker, Dennis Riggs, Bob Taylor, Jeri Swinton, Trish Pugh Jones, John Clark, Julia Parke, and Matilda Andrews. Those, plus the founding director, Kevin Connelly, were joined by the deft planning direction of Doug Stegner, and early board chairs, Stan Siegwald and Dale Josey.

Kevin Connelly, our CEO, extends a special thanks to CNPE's staff members, who have consistently brought exceptionally high levels of talent and dedication to advance the mission for a strengthened social sector. For each of them, let the excellence showcased in the pages that follow serve as evidence of their much valued and appreciated contributions: Jennifer Lose, Bo Manning, Judy Schroeder, Tobby Spalding, Sharron Akin, Stephanie Spriegler, Heather Parrino, Susan

O'Neil, Alina Pabin, Vanessa Johnson, Emily Beauregard and the current team of Darlene Whitney, Eric Schmall, Désirée Jones, and Merv Antonio.

Our current location at ArtSpace represents an exciting phase in our journey; we acknowledge Allan Cowen and the Fund for the Arts for their vision of this creative collaboration.

For the production and publication of *Striving for Excellence in the Social Sector: A Decade of Distinction*, we wish to acknowledge the support of the following foundations:

    Anonymous

    Community Foundation of Southern Indiana

    C. E. & S. Foundation

    Community Foundation of Louisville

    Cralle Foundation

    Humana Foundation

AUTHOR'S ACKNOWLEDGEMENT

I am grateful for the opportunity to catalogue these stories and remind the sector about the importance of these characteristics of excellence. I wish to express my gratitude to the board of directors for their authorization to pursue this work and the strong and sure direction given to me by CNPE's CEO, Kevin Connelly.

I want to express thanks to the specific individuals who allowed me time to meet with them in order to update and more fully understand their accomplishments as related in each chapter's Spotlight section. These generous people include, Gordon Brown, President and CEO of Home of the Innocents; Cynthia Knapek, Executive Director of Brightside; Lynn Huffman, Executive Director of Gallapalooza, Inc.; Lynnie Meyer, Chief Development Officer of Norton Healthcare; Gail Becker, retired Executive Director of the Louisville Science Center; Jennifer Bielstein, Managing Director of Actors Theater of Louisville; Alexander "Sandy" Spear, retired Managing Director of Actors Theater of Louisville; and Edgardo Mansilla, Executive Director of Americana Community Center.

Finally, and in greatest measure, I express my thanks to my wife, Barbara, for her inexhaustible gifts of encouragement, patience, and insight as I composed this work.

CENTER FOR NONPROFIT EXCELLENCE

CONTENTS

Foreword *i*

Preface *v*

Introduction *vii*

1 The Art of Vision *1*

2 The Art of Leadership *19*

3 The Art of Governance *37*

4 The Art of Collaboration *65*

5 The Art of Diversity *85*

6 The Next Decade *105*

About the Author *109*

About the Center for Nonprofit Excellence (CNPE) *110*

References *111*

Praise for CNPE *113*

FOREWORD

The past ten years have been the best of times and the worst of times. Few would have predicted that the economy would go from rapid growth to a recession. As a result, there were high hopes for the community and the social service sector at the start of the decade (2000-2010).

The Center for Nonprofit Excellence (CNPE) was established to help the social sector—including those that provide human services, the arts, and education—to become better in terms of governance, leadership, management and, of course, fiscal responsibility. There are more than 1,600 groups providing services to individuals, families and communities in the Metro Louisville region. CNPE identified a myriad of training and consulting opportunities that would make the organizations and agencies stronger. Thus, a membership was built to create a capacity for these groups to be more effective and more efficient.

Along the way, funders expressed dismay over the inability to adequately address the requests for financial support. Many people expressed a perception of duplication and overlap, and there were some who thought that our community had too many social service entities. Thus, CNPE responded with a research initiative that would help us better understand the breadth and depth of social services in the region. This work included benchmarking our community with the same peers that are used in economic assessments.

Funders, agency heads, and the general public became more aware of community needs and how we were addressing them. As a result, CNPE developed a series of accountability measures so that investments in the organizations and agencies as well as the outcomes of their work could be better articulated. People were impressed with how efficient the social services sector was in delivering needed services. And, they had the data to prove it!

In the latter part of this decade, the economy recoiled and immediately there were two reactions. First, the demand for social services increased dramatically as people lost jobs, families lost homes, and more people were unable to secure the basics of food, healthcare and social support. Second, support for all categories within the sector was diminished. Those who had been generous cut back or withdrew because of their own circumstances. Thus, many of the gains in community social services were challenged. CNPE responded with seminars, workshops, and consulting designed to help organization and agency leaders deal with the economic realities. While CNPE was also experiencing some challenges, initiatives for helping the sector were often presented at little or no cost to ensure everyone had the ability to continue growing in form and substance.

The joy of being a part of CNPE is to be aware of those individuals and organizations that have excelled over the years. Their creativity and boldness resulted in new ways to see the problems and better options for solving those problems. To recognize the possibilities and the outcomes, CNPE has given the Pyramid Awards of Excellence for outstanding contributions in governance, vision, leadership, collaboration, and diversity. Each year, there are many nominations made for these five awards. Often, it is hard to identify the "best" one where many stand out. Nonetheless, award winners are selected and celebrated at the CNPA Annual Conference.

In this book, Eric Schmall chronicles the award winners. His reviews are important and I hope you will read them. From the work of our winners come the ideas, tools, and processes that can be replicated in other settings and organizations. Equally important, you will discover the treasures that exist in our regional social service organizations and agencies, better understanding how they truly make a difference in the quality of all lives in our community.

All of this was possible because of the CNPE leadership and staff. Kevin Connelly sets the standard for expectations and ethics. A dedicated staff has worked to be creative and passionate in delivering services. And the board has been extraordinary in providing governance, insight, and support to the organization.

Now, sit back and discover for yourself why our community has witnessed exceptional performance in each of the sector's dimensions of social services—arts, humanities, education, health, human services, and community development.

Robert L. Taylor
Board Chair, Center for Nonprofit Excellence

PREFACE

In the opening chapter of his history of the Gallic Wars, Julius Caesar simplified things by explaining, "All Gaul is divided into three parts...." Allow me to follow his example by similarly dividing all of American society into three sectors: the public, (representing the various aspects of federal, state, and local government), the private (including all for-profit enterprises from sole proprietors to international corporations), and the "nonprofit" (organizations that exist substantially for some public benefit).

There are nearly 30 different types of nonprofits defined by the IRS, all of which are exempt for federal taxation, but most people know and support the predominant form, identified by the IRS code as "charitable" or defined as "501(c)(3)" organizations in their governmental parlance. These charitable organizations differ from all the other classifications in that they must: (1) benefit the broad public purpose, not just "members," and (2) must serve the community in areas designated as charitable, religious, educational, scientific, literary, testing for public safety, promoting the arts, fostering national or international amateur sports competition, or the prevention of cruelty to children or animals. Of the nearly 1.4 million registered nonprofit organizations in this nation, 64 percent fall into this category.

In this work I will abstain from the using the term "nonprofit" for two reasons. First, as was stated by Peter Block, a well-regarded author and business consultant who spoke at one of CNPE's annual conferences several years ago, "It's really a shame that this sector defines itself by proclaiming what it is *not*." The second reason rests upon the fact that the term "nonprofit" is at its core, an IRS tax designation, and not a business plan. A so-called "nonprofit" is not prohibited from ending its fiscal year with excess cash in the bank; it doesn't have to "zero-out" in its budget with no leftover money for a reserve fund. In fact, well-run nonprofits are defined by operating so wisely and efficiently that they purposely maintain reserves as a hedge against leaner times.

I will use the alternate term of "social profit" in lieu of "nonprofit," a term suggested by Claire Guadiani in an article of *The Journal of Philanthropy* ("Let's Put the Word 'Nonprofit' Out of Business," July 26, 2007). I believe her suggestion most vividly captures the true spirit of charitable enterprises and those who endeavor to bring about improvements in all communities. The real benefits they all propose to offer to the community come from addressing social needs, eliminating community problems (poverty, illness, etc.), or fulfilling community cultural desires (arts, historic preservation, recreation). For the more general term that includes all the social profits in the sector, I'll employ the simpler phrase "social sector" as Jim Collins used in his monograph, *Good to Great in the Social Sectors*.

INTRODUCTION

In 1998, social profit leaders in the metropolitan area of Louisville, Kentucky were searching for ways in which they could improve their organizations' ability to become successful in pursuit of mission. They wanted to build their skills in fund development, develop their staff's knowledge and competencies, strengthen board governance, and establish a resource to help them think strategically.

The local foundations and Metro United Way wanted to see social profit boards become more adept at their fiscal oversight and leadership. They were willing to fund social profits' education, but there was no one single recognized educational resource toward which to guide them. The local Metro United Way called for a greater understanding and practical application of methods that would clearly demonstrate social sector impact and outcomes.

Ultimately, all of these conversations led to further research into what other cities were doing to resolve these issues. The search was on for a prototypical model of an organization that could address all of these needs. Generically called a "management support organization" (MSO), the envisioned entity would have these characteristics:

- Become established and governed as a social profit entity itself
- Offer its services to social profits in the Louisville Metro area and surrounding counties, including neighboring counties across the Ohio river in Southern Indiana

- Provide education and consulting to the social sector community in areas needed to build their capacity to achieve mission
- Model and promulgate a culture of community collaboration, adaptation, and learning

In 1999, the Donors Forum of Metropolitan Louisville (composed of 37 area foundations), working with the Metro United Way, the Gheens and Horn foundations, the City of Louisville, and Bellarmine College (now Bellarmine University), created a new independent agency to support the social sector in the Louisville, Kentucky region.

The Center for Nonprofit Excellence (CNPE) came into being in February 1999 after securing start-up funding and designing a means by which this group could become economically self-sustaining—principally through two means: (1) earned revenue (membership and fees for educational and consulting services to its members) and (2) traditional means of fund development such as grants, corporate gifts, and donations. It pledged itself from that moment to fulfill its mission of "offering information, helping nonprofits realize their mission and achieve excellence."

From the very outset the founding board and CNPE's newly appointed executive director, Kevin Connelly, reflected upon the fundamental principles of how excellence in pursuit of mission could be realized and celebrated within the sector. They decided that CNPE would sponsor an annual conference calling all of its subscribers to participate in a day of learning, reflection, and commemoration of outstanding examples of social profits' behaviors that lead to mission success.

This formative group selected five key performance areas that represented what they considered were essential for this community's social sector, ones that would ultimately lead to vibrant, sustaining mission success for every organization. These five proclaimed "arts" are:
- Art of Vision
- Art of Leadership
- Art of Governance
- Art of Collaboration
- Art of Diversity

Aside from using these topics as core areas to offer in its educational and consulting expertise, the founders wanted to emphasize these topics in another unique way. CNPE would invite social profit organizations to submit examples of how they saw success achieved through exemplary performance in these selected categories. At its annual conference every fall, CNPE would honor the one social profit in each category that best represented excellence in each subject area as a means of re-enforcing these ideals and inspiring the rest of the social profit community to model these successes.

In recognition of CNPE's tenth annual conference this year in 2010, this book proposes to offer three significant values. The first of these will be to explore each of these five specific Arts—Vision, Leadership, Governance, Collaboration, and Diversity—in more depth. All of these concepts represent crucial areas that the social sector must act upon in order to achieve excellence. Clarity around what is meant by excellence in each of these categories is, therefore, always appropriate. Second, this anniversary offers us an opportunity to look back upon our progress in the sector, reflecting upon those recognized organizations and encourage us all on the potential achievements that these examples of excellence offer. Third, out of all the decade's achievements in each category, we wanted to select at least one of those award recipients in each category (in the Governance section we actually decided to showcase two different award winners) for a more in-depth look at their story and see what other lessons they have to offer the community.

The final chapter faces forward toward the next decade and the need to expand recognition into two new categories that will be key in helping the sector confront and overcome the challenges ahead: the Art of Innovation and the Art of Generating New Leadership.

The Art of Vision

CHAPTER 1

If I were to wish for anything I should not wish for wealth and power, but for the passionate sense of what can be, for the eye, which ever young and ardent, sees possible. Pleasure disappoints, possibility, never. And what wine is so sparkling, what so fragrant, what so intoxicating as possibility?
—Søren Kierkegaard

It always begins with the dream. The dream jolts us out of our complacence; it disrupts our acceptance of what we have told ourselves comprises the hardship of life. Poverty, hunger, disease, war, ignorance, the exploitation of the weak by the powerful, all are just part of the human condition, we grimly remind ourselves. But the dream intrudes, insisting that these are not inevitable and irreversible aspects of the human experience. In fact, if we were to conceive of them as not so much as inevitable, but simply *unacceptable*, we take the first critical step toward engendering change.

Robert Greenleaf, the author who created the concept of servant-leadership, has made this observation about such dreams: "The test of greatness of a dream is that it has the energy to lift people out of their moribund ways to a level of being and relating from which the future can be faced with more hope than most of us can summon today."

The quality Greenleaf describes shows how vision/dreams snap people into a higher awareness. Suddenly people are "awakened" and infused with hope of achieving this better world.

A vision describes an idealized future, one that brims with hope and possibilities. It not only represents the potential of the social profit organization, but more importantly how the community—or whole world—can become better, thanks to the relentless efforts of that organization to inspire others, galvanize support, and ultimately work to bring about a better future.

VISIONS ARE EVERYWHERE

All humans are animated by dreams of a better future. All who envision better circumstances find renewed energy through the hope of such things as a more fulfilling job, achieving a long-sought goal, improving oneself in a valued way. But the dreams don't just stop with the individual.

At this very moment, someone in a town somewhere is sitting at her kitchen table thinking that the local neighborhood so long beset by litter and encroaching vandalism, doesn't *have* to be that way. Right now a group of parents whose children are dealing with some rare, devastating childhood infirmity are resolved that they will no longer accept the fact that no support can be found or created to help treat the disease. At present, a retired business professional is dreaming of how a rundown abandoned building might become converted into a theater for children in an area of the city that has never before had such a resource before.

These people are ordinary citizens, not powerfully rich or politically well-connected. They aren't necessarily brighter or more gifted than anyone else, but they do possess the magic of harnessing the power of an idealized, better future. If they can communicate their passion and stir within others the same zeal, everything can change.

Thirty years ago, California mother Candy Lightner was given the devastating news about the death of her thirteen year-old daughter, Cari, killed by a repetitively convicted DWI driver. Two days after her daughter's funeral, that aggrieved mother resolved to start a movement to combat this outrageous irresponsibility so that no other parent would ever have to suffer this kind of loss again. That movement became

Mothers Against Drunk Driving (MADD) which, subsequently, has had a profound change on our nation and culture.

This woman had no extraordinary innate talent to make history change, but she did have the determination and unrelenting vision to awaken people to the needless loss that was occurring by not addressing the issues of drinking and driving.

In her case, as in all other social profits, the emergent potential for significant change came into being through an inspired vision; in each case, an alternate envisioned brighter, better future is waiting to be born.

Power of Vision

Visions inspire political movements and propel nations and peoples into whirlwinds of change. Visions affect us intellectually, but more importantly at our emotional core. People are willing to sacrifice their lives and fortunes when they become enraptured by a vision.

Similar to the power of the atom, the power of vision itself is morally neutral. Visions can be used to usher in an age of harmony or unleash unspeakable wickedness. Rev. Martin Luther King Jr.'s vision of how humans should live together represents the polar opposite of someone like Osama Bin Laden. Yet in each case these historical figures used the power of vision to inspire their followers to act and profoundly change history.

Vision in Organizations

Any group organized to perform a task has some form of vision that explains the essence of why they exist, the purpose of their working together.

In general, governments exist with a vision of providing public order and protection of its citizenry. Our own Constitution starts out with this visionary clarity about why the United States wanted to form a national government: ". . . in order to form a more perfect union, establish justice, insure domestic tranquility, provide for the common defense, promote the general welfare, and secure the blessings of liberty to ourselves and our posterity . . ."

In the for-profit sector, business enterprises all have a common vision: to increase the wealth of the owner(s). Whether that be through encoding software, building cars, providing hotel accommodations or banking services, all of those are simply means to the one envisioned future: at the end of the day, or fiscal quarter, or year—to make more money than they are spending and distributing that increased wealth (profits) to the owners.

In great contrast, in the social sector, every organization has a fundamentally distinct vision, unique to it as our own DNA is to each of us. That vision can be as modest as a neighborhood's intention to make its three-square block area, a safe, clean, and attractive living space for all its families. Or it can be as bold as the American Cancer Society's vision—creating a world where someday cancer no longer plagues humankind.

Need for Vision in Non-Profits

Dr. Rick Warren's runaway mega-seller *Purpose Driven Life* demonstrates the deep inner need for all humans to ponder the question of the "why" of their existence. The same profound requirement exists within each social profit. People have to connect to the ultimate question about the purposeful good the organization hopes to bring into being. Author Simon Sinak in his work *Start With Why* has notably advanced the concept, even in the for-profit world that "People don't buy *what* you do; they buy *why* you do it. And what you do serves as the proof of what you believe."

Visions are born from values and principles. If one believes in a principle that children's nutritional health is not merely the responsibility of their parents—that somehow the entire community has some role to play so as to insure that no child has to experience hunger—then that fundamental belief can readily be translated into this kind of vision: "We want to create a community where no child has to go to bed hungry." It means that the organization believes that it is wrong if any one child in the city suffers hunger, that there is a collective responsibility to remove that wrong.

A clearly articulated, vibrant vision inspires people to act in ways that will bring about mission success in the social sector. It drives people to volunteer, donate, and offer their leadership—as for example, by serving on the board of directors. It motivates staff to work long hours for pay considerably lower than they might gain in the for-profit sector. It awakens within the corporate community a deeper sense of civic responsibility and moves them to a greater desire to participate in giving help.

Sometimes a vision will be used to describe what the organization itself must become in order to bring about the ideal future. In that case, the vision focuses on the characteristics of the organization and connects those attributes to the needs of those whom the social profit serves. So this kind of vision might be framed as ". . . in delivering food to those in need, we will become the most effective and efficient food bank in the southwest region." As helpful as this may be, it is still incomplete. While it may be well to imagine the idealized organization, the most important vision must dwell on the consequential benefit that the community will enjoy as a result of developing this great organization.

Vision Differs from Mission

Confusion often arises over the difference between vision and mission. If vision is focused upon the idealized future—the world that *could* be realized and toward which we should move—then mission is all about *what* the organization does and *for whom* it is done in order to bring about that envisioned future. Mission statements are always written down—in fact, it is a fundamental core document that is required in any social sector organization's application process. Mission statements describe the actions that will occur (e.g., create, provide, build, preserve, improve, eliminate, protect, heal, educate) so that the vision will be achieved. In other words, missions are all about the verb.

In stark contrast, however, vision statements are less frequently written down or given clear unified definition. This can be catastrophic. Visions are sustained only by constant re-articulation; people have to keep reminding themselves of the great and wonderful cause, the ideal world they are working to bring about.

If a group collectively loses the ability to describe for themselves and to others the ultimate end-state they're pursing (e.g., "world-class contemporary theater productions in our community"), they will ultimately be unable to make compelling sense of what needs to be accomplished. Lack of focus will cripple any attempts to set goals, enlist support, and move confidently into the future. An unarticulated vision, an idealized story that is no longer told about the future, leads to a lost organization.

CNPE's Vision Award Concepts

The founding CNPE leadership realized the core importance of the power of vision as it formed its first discussions of the abiding principles of excellence. As it developed the guiding characteristics of what it means to meet the criteria of the Art of Vision, the team promoted several major themes, which have remained consistent over time.

The first of these was that the collective vision was one which appealed to people and offered a means to inspire others to act in response. Visions strike a resonant chord in the heart. Tell someone who already cares about humane treatment of animals how your pet shelter has a "no-kill' policy and is dedicated to placing every dog and cat into a caring home, and you can count on very favorable emotional response. Visions connect people to basic shared values and awaken within them the inspiration to support such ideals through donations of time and other resources.

The second principle states that the vision logically connects to and brings unity to the mission and programs. As an example, consider the American Heart Association vision, one where cardiovascular disease is eliminated in this nation. The core of their mission statement is "to build healthier lives, free of cardiovascular disease and strokes." It accomplishes this through education, research, and advocacy programs.

The third critical vision component rests on the principle that it has to have some relevance to community need. Having a solid grasp of the principal beneficiaries of the vision and staying in constant awareness of their changing needs keeps the vision in a dynamic and adaptive mode. For example, the needs of the poor in a community as they may have been defined in the early twentieth century do not necessarily match the needs of the poor as they present themselves in 2010. The vision has to adapt to changing characteristics.

The final component in judging the Art of Vision is the demonstration that the vision and mission have led to some real, tangible community benefits. Visions must be converted into real and tangible actions and results.

Few things are as tragic in the social sector than witnessing an organization whose heart is in the right place (i.e., solid, clear vision and mission) and yet has not demonstrated the ability to accomplish any progressive movement toward accomplishing those ideals. The bottom line for all social profit groups can only be described in terms of mission success. These have to be shown in the forms of demonstrable change, not just anchored in meaningless program data that merely indicates activity, with no evidence of results. For example, if a social profit organization only shows proof of a great deal of activity, say, of offering smoking cessation classes, but cannot show any evidence that those classes have led to permanent behavior change, and consequentially, better health, one might reasonably conclude that their mission is not being achieved.

The collective force of all of the elements—the unifying effect of an aligned vision and mission, deeply rooted in community need, and effective in bringing about demonstrable change sums up what the Art of Vision promotes and promulgates.

Section II

A Decade of Vision Award Recipients

Louisville Science Center, 2001
(See Spotlight, Section III, p. 15)

Heuser Hearing Institute, 2002
Sometimes a vision means moving toward larger horizons, expanding to a wider geography of service, offering richer programs and reaching for national recognition as a result of successful impact. In 2002, CNPE recognized these attributes in the Heuser Hearing Institute—which was born out of the operational history of Louisville Deaf Oral School. The board envisioned creating a "Center of Excellence," a nationally recognized, unique provider of comprehensive hearing health care for

both children and adults who experience hearing loss. This vision brought them to establish the Heuser Hearing Institute. This new 501(c)(3) was established after a $6.5 million dollar campaign was concluded and a $2 million dollar partnership set up with the University of Louisville, Jewish Hospital HealthCare Services, and Norton Healthcare Systems.

The Heuser Hearing Institute is unique in the United States, incorporating diagnostics, providing ear-related medical services, cochlear implants, assisted living devices for those with hearing loss, ear-related medical service, and nationally funded hearing-related research.

The power of the board's vision, to transform a limited, though historically successful agency, to new and higher realms of service and performance to a larger community of those in need is an outstanding example of how a group can take a dream and move it to an inspiring reality.

YouthBuild of Louisville, 2003

Vision inspires others to come to your assistance, especially if you can link it to other community dreams. In 2003, CNPE recognized YouthBuild of Louisville for that very reason. YouthBuild is a dynamic community and youth development program started in East Harlem in 1978. The model program is designed to help young people rebuild their own difficult lives through their participation in physically constructing housing for low-income families and participating in classes in order to finish high school or earn their GED. Under the director of Lynn Rippy, YouthBuild of Louisville came into being in the late 1990s with the collaborative engagement and help of over 50 local agencies and businesses. This kind of support can only be derived from a clearly defined vision, one that others can embrace at an emotional and intellectual level, and motivate them to contribute in any way they can. More importantly, YouthBuild was able to link its ardent devotion to helping rebuild lives to a 2002 Brooking Institute vision report regarding Louisville needs. That report called for strengthening educational attainment for students, especially the lowest–achieving ones. In addition, the report recommended "making neighborhood investment strategies integral to its education reform agenda." YouthBuild's clear linkage of its vision to that strongly indentified need for improved community continues to inspire support of their mission success.

Junior Achievement of Kentuckiana, 2004

Visions, once they get themselves established, always have a need to grow. That was the case in point for the 2004 Vision award that went to Junior Achievement of Kentuckiana. Over 50 years, JA has had the mission of improving children's lives through teaching, practical experience, and personal role modeling. While initially proud of their outreach in touching the lives of 18 percent of the student population by 2002, the board challenged the organization by asking the vital question "What about the other 82 percent?"

Thus was born the expanded vision of reaching every child in greater Louisville and Southern Indiana with plans to realign its resources to reach all students four different times in the school career—in the third, fifth, and eighth grades, and once in high school. Junior Achievement of Kentuckiana became a pioneer in the nation in adopting this bold, broadened vision. Linking this extremely ambitious vision to the region's deeply felt needs for workforce development, this vision inspired partnerships to finance expanding JA's operational programs and facilities in order to bring this dream into reality.

Habit for Humanity of Metro Louisville, 2005

With each step that brings one closer to vision, excitement and optimism builds—and leads to dreaming a larger dream. Habitat for Humanity of Metro Louisville's mission is to build simple, decent houses in partnership with God's people in need. It was founded in 1985 and 20 years later had built 217 homes sheltering 242 adults and 447 children with only 2 foreclosures. Habitat Family Services qualifies, selects, and provides a family nurture program to enable low-income families to become successful homeowners.

Habitat has connected its vision of simple, decent houses and partner family support to community priorities. They are replacing abandoned weed-choked lots in neighborhoods in distress with beautiful, energy efficient, affordable homes. The property values in the neighborhoods are increasing; children and their parents are thriving in a safe place where they can grow, dream and set new goals.

In 1999, Habitat completed its 100th house and determined to double production in five years to build "100 More by 2004." They met that goal on September 18, 2004. That goal inspired and challenged them to complete their 300th house in Louisville by 2009 (and they did!).

And the expanding dreams goes on to this very day. Rob Locke, executive director, reflecting the on-going vision, stated, "We took 24 years to build our first 300 homes and we want to build 300 more in less than ten (years); we call it building the dream of 2019."

The Healing Place, 2006

One of the most difficult aspects of creating a vision is in its very formation. Is it too ambitious? Is it too unorthodox? Has it any chance of success? This was the part of The Healing Place's story.

It is the mission of The Healing Place to provide shelter for the homeless and recovery for the addicted. The shelter's programs have been innovative in that they combine both a shelter that provides beds for the homeless—regardless of intoxication—as well as a substance-free detoxification center. In 1991, when Jay P. Davidson took the lead of The Healing Place, the board was sharply divided as to whether the shelter should be substance-free or open to all in need. Through his vision, Davidson helped to unite the board, leading to the development of an institution that has set a national precedent for recovery in shelter programs.

Part of The Healing Place vision is to have all mentoring and healing done by alumni of the program. This is not only cost effective, but has proven a highly effective method of treating the addicted. Reports have shown that 65 percent of The Healing Place graduates maintain sobriety for a year following the program—five times the national average for substance addiction recovery programs.

The US Department of Health and Human Services has given the program national recognition as "A Model That Works," and Dr. Burns Brady, a nationally known specialist in addiction medicine, said that "The Healing Place is the best recovery program in the world."

The Healing Place saves an estimated 3.5 million dollars in annual jail and hospital expense—one million dollars more than the program's own annual budget. More importantly, it saves lives. The vision is animated by two fundamental convictions: every person has a right to a home and every person has a right to recovery from alcoholism and addiction. From those convictions, the vision is manifested.

Women 4 Women, 2007

Visions connect many conceptual dots in communities. By improving one aspect of our society, other benefits flourish. But you have to recognize those connecting intersections to inspire support.

Women 4 Women envisions our community as one of the best places for girls, women and their families to live and work.

Women 4 Women concentrates on programs that will produce long-term benefits for women and girls in Metro Louisville. In 1999, Cissy Musselman and other community leaders came together to start the work needed to improve the health and economic well-being of women and girls by increasing awareness, expanding resources, and creating solutions to strengthen the entire community. The connecting vision: By strengthening women, entire families are made more successful and self-sufficient, allowing them to give back to the community.

The *Benchmark 2000* research project determined that significant improvements needed to be made in the areas of economic well-being, health, connections, and funding for women's programming and services. This led to specific programs that focus now upon women's financial literacy, fitness and nutrition education for underserved, at-risk middle school girls, and a structured networking program for women and girls from all areas of the community to learn about problem solving and sharing knowledge of helpful resources.

Women 4 Women continues to show proven beneficial linkage "connections" between participants. *The Fund 4 Women and Girls* has been established at The Community Foundation of Louisville to support this vital work. Women 4 Women's board and staff continue their program creativity that provides resources to improve women's lives as well as their families.

Teach Kentucky, 2007

Visions rely upon bringing the best resources to produce the best results. That was certainly the theme of 2007's tying award winner for the Art of Vision.

Teach Kentucky founders' vision looks to a public school system in which all students are taught by highly skilled, knowledgeable, and dedicated teachers. The program is unique in building collaborative relationships between local school districts and the University of Louisville College of Education and Human Development to construct a coherent method to attract young candidates. Traditionally, school districts draw applicants from those currently living in the area. Teach Kentucky increases this pool by recruiting efforts on campuses beyond the traditional institutions.

Teach Kentucky has brought a number of teachers from over 20 highly selective national colleges and universities. Virtually all of them serve in middle schools, the majority teaching in hard-to-fill math and science positions.

Once again, the vision does not stand alone, but demonstrates that it can become a key aspect of a larger vision shared by others. Metro Louisville is striving to improve its standing in comparison to competitor cities, most notably through the Greater Louisville Project. Teach Kentucky assists in this effort by bringing promising young professionals into the community to improve the education of the children within the public school system.

Fund for the Arts, 2008

Artists and their creations are perfect examples of the power of vision. Art can unleash the creativity that animates our public life, helps cultivate our connection to meaning that transcends uncertain times, and serves to support our economic well-being.

In its 59th year supporting Louisville's world-class arts and cultural organizations, the Fund for the Arts earned Louisville the designation, "Best in Support of the Arts in the U.S." by having the largest dollar increase of any united arts fund campaign in the U.S. in 2008. In addition, with the support of the Louisville community, the Fund raised and contributed the highest dollar amount in its history. A 2008 campaign total of $9,165,200 provided increased allocations to Fund member groups and allowed for significant increases to the Teacher Arts Grant and Community Arts Grant programs.

Having a vision about resource development is only one aspect of the Fund for Arts' vision prowess. It also had a dream of finding a way of driving the efficiencies of the many art groups in the metro area. In 2008, the Fund for the Arts also celebrated the one-year anniversary of the new and highly successful ArtSpace—a mixed-use social profit and arts incubator that has provided administrative space for numerous Fund for the Arts' member groups and other community social profit organizations—from the University of Louisville to the Center for Nonprofit Excellence. ArtSpace has already encouraged creative collaboration and synergies, including new social profit technology programs providing hands-on experience for University of Louisville students and much needed technology assistance for the social sector.

Hand in Hand Ministries, 2009

Visions may evolve over time—or they may strike with one life changing, searing moment of experience or insight. In November 1994, Hand in Hand Ministries co-founder Wayne Fowler visited Kingston, Jamaica, and his experience there forever transformed his life. He visited orphanages where he met children so badly handicapped that they were unable to shoo the flies from their faces. However, it was not only the children and conditions that greatly affected Fowler; it was the tens of thousands of children and families living in hovels made of zinc, cardboard and pieces of wood that wouldn't pass for a doghouse in the United States.

Wayne found it impossible to put the experience behind him and felt he had to do something. Five years later, Hand In Hand Ministries was created to work with the poorest of the poor in Central America, the Caribbean and, eventually, the United States.

In each location where this ministry works, it has searched out the community's needs through formal and informal advisory boards and sought to build programs that respond to those needs. Their Building for Change program in Belize City, Belize, provides a modest 15x16 foot wooden home for families and the elderly to replace their vermin-infested shanties. They have built over 120 homes since 2001, and have 20 more scheduled for 2010, with between 500-1000 applications from those looking for decent housing. The Pathway to Change program seeks to address the lack of educational opportunities afforded children who live in barrios near the city garbage dump and who would otherwise drop out by the fifth grade.

It is never easy working in underserved communities, especially when they're outside your own country, but Hand in Hand Ministries gives it their all. They provide dignity and hope when there seemingly is none. Their work and success is a testament to the organization, its leadership and compelling vision that best exemplifies how much one can accomplish with limited resources, strong will, and enduring grace.

EDGE OUTREACH, 2010

As much as a noble vision might be proclaimed, sometimes it takes a tragedy to awaken people to its realization. EDGE OUTREACH envisions a world with access to clean water, free from waterborne diseases that cause 1.7 million deaths every year worldwide. EDGE OUTREACH trains, equips, and mobilizes ordinary people in sustainable solutions for clean water, health and hygiene, and sanitation, around the world. They work with individuals and organizations offering hands-on training in scalable water solutions and hand-pump repair. It accomplishes this mission by leading groups of volunteers from all over the country to post-disaster communities where they work alongside residents and leaders to install inexpensive, highly efficient water purification systems, conduct health and hygiene education, and minster to the needs of the community.

Early in 2010, the disastrous earthquake in Haiti prompted EDGE OUTREACH to answer its vision's call in a most profound way. EDGE demonstrated its prowess as a skilled first responder in delivering their water treatment to that wounded nation's devastated population.

This extraordinary response could not meet the demand without a deeper understanding in the Louisville community about EDGE OUTREACH's vision and the ways in which the population here could assist. Through local media coverage of EDGE OUTREACH's vision and mission, donations began to pour in; within weeks, over $500,000 flowed from individuals, organizations, and corporations to help EDGE and its dramatic water distillation delivery teams. Since initiating this response in Haiti, EDGE has installed 31 water purification systems, serving communities and villages of anywhere from 300-4,000 people, supplying them with the vital necessity of clean drinking water. And the dream grows yet today. EDGE will rise to its beckoning vision by installing 117 water purification systems in Haiti by the end of 2010, as well as training its population on water purification and maintaining those systems in order to build a sustained infrastructure of delivering clean water in that country.

Section III

SPOTLIGHT ON: ART OF VISION: LOUISVILLE SCIENCE CENTER, 2001

A superb example of how the power of vision can transform and energize a social profit organization toward ultimate mission success can be found in the story of the Louisville Science Center, winner of the Art of Vision Pyramid award in 2001.

In an interview with Gail Becker, the Center's executive director for seventeen years (1991-2008), she explained how that transformation hinged upon the board's relentless commitment to its vision.

The Louisville Science Center moved to its Main Street location in 1977 and grew its capacity over that next decade, principally by adding an IMAX theater to its property in 1988. But still the Science Center struggled financially as well as programmatically in drawing people in as active visitors and involved participants in experiencing the wonders of science.

However, beginning in 1991—when the board hired Gail as its new executive director—the governing board started developing a refreshed vision of what the Louisville Science Center could become to the region. Through a long process of intense board sessions, the board focused on what the facility could offer, what its primary purpose should be, and how it could most effectively improve the public's understanding of science, mathematics, and technology. As a direct result, the board developed a three-phase plan of installing permanent exhibits, each of which would take on unique scientific themes. The first, called "The World We Create," was a celebration of creative thinking and supported by 40 exhibits—it became a resounding success. It was followed by the next phase, entitled "The World Within Us," that has life sciences and health themes. That phase similarly attracted significantly more attendees and membership support. The last phase, "The World Around Us," examines natural and earth sciences and builds upon the two earlier popular phases.

The purpose of these evolving permanent exhibits was to move the Louisville Science Center toward the board's envisioned dream of establishing the largest and most experientially influential science center in Kentucky and surrounding region. The board knew that it would have to prove the vision's worth as well as the leadership's competence to bring about this future, so they deliberately orchestrated the vision to unfold in those well-identified phases over a number of years.

Using this vision to excite and inspire major funders in the region to help underwrite the extensive plan, the board linked the Center's mission of delivering education in the realms of physical, natural, and biological sciences to Kentucky's Education Reform Act (KERA). The purpose of KERA was to enhance the state's approach to more effective public school education. As each phase of the planned exhibits attracted more visitors, teachers, and students, and drew more accolades, the board's vision and its appeals for more financial support from area foundations grew.

The board recognized that it required ways in which to gauge its visionary success. Over the years, the telling signs made themselves evident: school visits from every county in Kentucky, funding from the National Science Foundation, increased family memberships, and vastly increased the numbers of people touched by the Louisville Science Center experience. The number of visitors—both to the Center and its "touring" exhibits—expanded from 300,000 to over 500,000 annually.

"You have to have the vision to capture everyone's imagination, and then you have to have a strategic plan." Gail explained. The vision had to have a unifying effect for the board, staff, and eventually the donor community for the dream to become realized. Gail brought her own expertise and knowledge about creating and staging permanent exhibits to the process and educated the board on the importance these have in quest of a delivering an educational experience in a museum setting. "The board listened carefully and conducted extended meetings about the vision and plan," she recounted. "They were faithful about revisiting the plan every year and making revisions as we grew. But without a vision about where we wanted to go, none of our success would have been possible."

The Art of Leadership

CHAPTER 2

"You see things; and you say, 'Why?' But I dream things that never were; and I say, "Why not?"
—George Bernard Shaw

Vision alone cannot bring about transformation. Visions need to be proclaimed and acted upon. Leaders articulate the vision and spark within others the desire to bring about that ideal future.

Jim Kouzes and Barry Posner in their seminal book, *The Leadership Challenge,* specify that envisioning the future is one of the key components of effective leadership, saying that such leaders can "see" across the horizon of time and describe the ideal time to come. Exemplary leaders excite and inspire others to join them in the quest. These leaders center their passion upon bringing that envisioned world into reality. Most tellingly, leaders understand that the realization of the dream far surpasses what it may mean for them. As Dr. Martin Luther King, Jr. fatefully foretold his audience on the night before his assassination: "And I've seen the Promised Land. I may not get there with you. But I want you to know tonight, that we, as a people, will get to the Promised Land!"

Leaders not only paint the picture of the idealized future, they stimulate the faith in that dream and engender hope in their followers.

Even as improbable as it may seem now, just by describing what the future could be—a city without poverty, a world without cancer, a community where world-class creative artistic endeavors occur—stimulates irresistible hope. Leadership promises, promotes, encourages, and gives rise to collective voice. This became very evident in the 2008 presidential campaign when so many voters were moved to participate by the phrase: "Yes we can."

Leadership emerges in this social profit sector with a distinct egalitarian flair to it. Any person can don the mantle of leadership after making the decision to bring about some improvement to the world. Ordinary citizens may become founding members of any social profit, determined to bring about a change, driven by a dream, and ready to enlist others with their inspiring tales of possibilities.

In that original state, the founding leaders may not possess much more than a vision in terms of resources. The skeptical world will often respond with disdain or disbelief: "So you folks are the ones who will end violence in this city?" "Oh, so you think producing Shakespeare performances in prisons will somehow transform lives?" "Let me get this straight—you think we can reach international peace through disarmament?" In each case, the challenging reaction can be summed up as: "Who are you to bring about this kind of change?"

Who, indeed? Napoleon once notably remarked about the widespread potential of leadership within his army, "Every French private carries a marshal's baton in his knapsack." So too do the inspired ordinary citizens of any community who band together to bring a dream into reality. And it can be manifested in many differing ways.

LEADERSHIP ≠ MANAGEMENT

Although these terms are often intertwined almost to the point where they may become indistinguishable, the terms "leadership" and "management" possess very different components, and in many ways can reflect diametrically different values.

Leadership arises from a vision, and excites and motivates to action. But practical action has to be carefully mapped out, and controlled, which is more a function of management. Leadership focuses on the disjoint between what is and what could be—and, from that differentiating tension, calls for change. Management, while imposing a necessary discipline for that change, acts more as a stabilizing influence and resists variation. People feel the need to be led, but generally resent being managed. Leadership, in its continuous call for what could be, is a disrupter of the status quo and wants to take the bold risks. Disruptions and risks are antithetical to management. Leadership lives in the creative realm, while management thrives on consistency as its favorite venue. True leadership engenders followers, ones who want to buy into the excitement of the envisioned future.

LEADERSHIP POWER

Extending leadership influence in the social profit arena varies quite a bit from the model people witness in the public or for-profit sectors. One of the prime differences comes from the understanding of why leaders have sought that role. As compared to the government or for-profit sectors, it's not about the vast potential political power that might emanate from that role, nor is it about gaining substantial personal wealth. No, these leaders are driven by the need to see their vision come into being through relentless and determined mission-based actions.

Given that social profit organizations are often fueled principally by cadres of volunteers, their leaders cannot issue commands as a general might to his adjutant staff, or as a CEO might exhort her employees to higher levels of productivity. Leadership and methods of communication in the social profit world take on a special nuance by necessity.

Jim Collins, in his monograph, *Good to Great and the Social Sectors* makes the very intriguing claim that the ultimate leadership characteristics (or "Level 5" in his parlance) are blends of personal devotion to the mission and personal humility that creates an atmosphere of legitimacy and influence by the leader. By demonstrating unerring devotion to bringing about mission success, and by abjuring the normal panoply of power and privilege, this kind of leader inspires and motivates like no other. People enlist to follow this kind of leader, not from fear, or envy, or promise of personal wealth, but rather for this deeper, exemplary promised world.

Collins goes on to offer the opinion that within the social profit world, leadership manifests itself in a more "legislative" manner rather than "executive." Executive power has a direct, formal, institutionalized positional authority to command. Legislative power, on the other hand, cannot be exercised by pure authority of position; it must act in a collegial, persuasive, and collaborative manner, demonstrating how common interests can be advanced through working together.

In this model, much depends upon the leader's exhibited devotion to values and integrity. Peter Drucker, the preeminent management and leadership scholar of the twentieth century, in his book, *The New Realities*, adds to Collins' basic concept saying that effective leaders can't succeed with passion alone; they have to make the competent decisions that will lead to ultimate mission success. Mission devotion without know-how and disciplined execution of the plan will not yield anything of value.

Essential Model—The Servant as Leader

No matter where one might play a role in a social profit organization—on the board, as the executive director, a staff member, or volunteer—the constant reminder of subservience to mission success and the demand to act as a leader in that service, brings the practitioner back to perhaps the most fundamental model of all in leadership, the *servant-leader*.

First offered by author Robert Greenleaf in his 1970 essay, "The Servant as Leader," and later expanded into the book *Servant Leadership*, this model best exemplifies the optimum spirit of leadership in the social profit sector. Drawing from very ancient wellsprings about leadership in Eastern and Western traditions, this form of leadership focuses on the concept of serving others first, then leading.

In the social profit world, this means putting the service of the mission and those who benefit from it as the top priority. The leadership component is driven by the ego's need for power and acquisition, but must be harnessed by the principles of service to the individuals at the epicenter of the cause. Anchored deep within the values and moral authority of the social good it wants to bring about, the leader keeps faith with the promise of mission success.

The servant-leader is other-directed. This leader listens, acts with empathy, compassion, and disciplined focus on results. This leader builds relationships, radiates connections in weaving wider circles of collaborative efforts empowers and emboldens others to act in concert with the mission. Through all of this effort, and as success grows, this leader only grows deeper humility and greater capacity to serve.

In the truest form of good governance, board members already embrace this kind of leadership. These board members know that service to mission comes first in their collective leadership and personal commitment. There should therefore, never be hesitation in knowing that all board members should contribute from their own personal wealth on a periodic basis to the organization. Nor will there be any doubt that every board member will offer to act in a capacity to bring in other resources, whether through soliciting funds from individuals, helping organize the annual fundraising event, or relentlessly asking local businesses for consideration of support. Equally important, this board will not flinch at the challenges brought on by recession-driven funding decreases, amplified by rising demands for services from their stakeholders. This board will still demand high performance results from the programs, demonstrating real evidence of steady movement toward mission success.

The board will set challenging standards of performance for the executive director and staff and the members will make themselves available to support all efforts to succeed. The board members put on the robes of governance at the board meetings to enact their promise as faithful stewards over the resources of the organization, and then after the meeting, put on quite different garments: the carpenter's apron and painter's cap, and help in assembling the booths for the annual festival.

Executive directors also will often display these servant-leader characteristics. These are the ones who would never ask the staff to do anything less than they would do in the relentless pursuit of mission. They model the behaviors they want to exhort in others, through demonstrating their sacrifice, passion, energy, and strict adherence to accountability for results. They are strong in their praise and soft in their criticism of those they lead.

CNPE's Leadership Award Concepts

The Art of Leadership Award has three concepts used in considering the ideal qualifying recipient.

Chief among these is the cohering connectivity between the leadership decisions and the mission and the values. No matter how noble the quest may be for the end vision by any social profit, each decision must be formed by a consistent application of the right choices and in the right spirit. This dimension re-emphasizes the aphorism that "Managers do *things right*, but leaders do the *right thing*."

Leaders inspire followers to join, act, and contribute. So the second dimension looks to the extent that the nominated leader demonstrates this level of support through engendering excitement and participation toward the promised goal. This should also be evident in the ways in which staff and volunteers are energized and participated to bring about success.

The final dimension concerns results. Galvanizing people to act should ultimately lead to real and tangible evidence of consistent mission results. It's never enough to simply engender wider support through better funding success or grow the volunteer base; these resources need to be channeled into meaningful impacts on the stakeholders—real evidence of mission-driven results, of really making an impact.

Section II

Art of Leadership Award Winners

J. Barry Barker, Executive Director, Transit Authority of River City (TARC), 2001

Leaders don't just wait or try to anticipate the future—they actually play a role in creating it through their inventiveness and persistence. J. Barry Barker (Barry) was named Executive Director of the Transit Authority of River City (TARC) in 1994. In the intervening time between his appointment to that position and the time of this award, Barry was responsible for establishing a team-based approach to management and training. He emphasized and directed that a customer-focused approach to restructuring service would be necessary to help achieve some of TARC's most valued mission outcomes: increased ridership and service innovations that would meet the ever-changing and complex public transportation challenges of a modern middle-sized American urban area, such as TARC's Access to Jobs initiatives.

Barry refuses to be limited by what others might consider to be boundaries when it comes to his creative leadership approach to solving complex problems. He is equally comfortable with widening the "big picture" to its maximum proportions to help others to achieve their goals. A prime example of this came about when Barry convened a group of social profits to discuss strategically creative ways that TARC could help with some of their clients' transportation requirements. Many of these other organizations had their own vans and buses—maintainance and upkeep of these assets represented a huge diversion of time and resources away from the core mission. Barry led the process to a point where they co-created a novel solution—a manner in which the agency transportation resources could be pooled and maintained by TARC, thus yielding two major benefits in one stroke: enormous overhead transport cost reductions for the agencies while giving TARC responsibilities it was most efficient and comfortable with—moving people effectively and efficiently and possessing top expertise in vehicle maintenance.

Barry recognized the role of his agency in being so integral to the good of the community; as a result, he has maintained a high leadership presence in the social sector. He has actively sought and successfully participated in numerous social profits as a very active board member, sharing his leadership talents in that way as well. He has been on the Metro United Way Board since 1995, and has chaired the Vital Neighborhoods Community Investment Team since its inception.

Lynnie Meyer, Executive Director, Center for Women and Families, 2002
(See Spotlight, Section III, p.34)

Joseph E. Gliessner, Jr., Executive Director, New Directions Housing Corporation 2003

Joe Gliessner joined New Directions Housing Corporation as executive director in 1986. He envisioned communities where families thrive, neighborhoods are safe, and talent is nurtured. During his tenure, he has served as project manager for the development of seven new apartment communities and overseen the partial renovation of numerous managed sites, thereby providing decent affordable housing for hundreds of families.

Neighborhood by neighborhood, Joe has demonstrated his capacity to recruit and organize diverse resources to make an important difference in the quality and supply of safe and affordable housing. He has leveraged his staff capacity by developing an army of volunteer resources. In the year of this award, over 1,400 volunteers gave nearly 9,000 hours of service.

Joe has served on a number of national and statewide advisory boards related to development and funding of affordable housing. His leadership on these boards continues to impact cities across the nation. On a regional level, his leadership has extended the influence of New Directions into three counties.

Joe's commitment to building a stronger community is firmly founded on the premise that safe, affordable housing is as important as clean air and water. His dedication and experience places Louisville on a short list of our nation's most innovative cities in the field of community development.

Denise Watts-Wilson, Executive Director of the LIGHT Center for Family Enrichment, 2004

Leadership can't always wait for followers. Following Gandhi's advice, they elect to "Be the change, you wish to see in others."

Denise was designated the winner in 2004 for her leadership in developing a summer food program for needy children in Oldham County, a program thought to be unfeasible and impossible to fund.

She mobilized an extensive volunteer force to position themselves in twelve locations around the community to receive and serve lunches to children in their own neighborhoods. Some of these sites had no shelter under which the meals could be served. This challenge did not deter Denise. She located the necessary resource funding and had five pavilions built to shelter the children at these meal sites. In addition, she developed recreational and instructional activities for the children. Some 230 low-to-middle income children were fed daily throughout the summer thanks to Denise's uncompromising determination to serve them.

Denise acted as the founder of this sponsoring organization, LIGHT Center for Family Enrichment, while at the same time maintaining her full-time occupation as a teacher in the Jefferson County school system. Her dedication to bringing meals to these children and marshalling the resources to operate the programs has inspired others to support her efforts. It has awakened in Oldham County a need that had not been readily recognized and certainly had not received formal volunteer support in the past.

Edgardo Mansilla, Executive Director, Americana Community Center 2005

Leaders are often founders in their creative visionary pursuits. These pursuits are often at odds with others' views and values. One key leadership challenge is found in how to engage and persuade others to see the good one intends to bring about. Edgardo Mansilla is an exemplary leader who has created a mission, vision and purpose for Americana Community Center (ACC). ACC has enabled the diverse residents of Metro Louisville to discover and utilize resources to build strong families, create a safe, supportive community and realize individual potential. Edgardo has been effective in rallying the community around the goals of ACC, to make its mission a reality.

Under his leadership, the ACC was moved in 2004 from a 2,500 square-foot facility to a 49,000 square-foot campus. It became the largest post-settlement agency for new Americans in Metro Louisville.

As is true with the challenges brought by leadership, Edgardo had to contend with opposition to his dream. He worked diligently to cultivate community partnerships and remove the fears people had about *new* citizens coming into the community.

He started two new programs: the Latino Police Academy, to educate Hispanic immigrants about how to relate to the police and a roundtable conversation for Africans and African-Americans. From these interactions, the participants became more appreciative of one another's culture, shared information and insight, and grew trusting relationships.

Edgardo's vision came to life in the Americana Festival when new citizens were sworn in outside the federal courtroom. Free tax services for low-income residents, Adult Education, a Girl Scout troop for Spanish speaking girls, a computer lab, art room, library, Kids Café and a recreation program are just some of the services his organization is providing to the community.

Edgardo has become a longstanding voice for diversity in this community with the courage and conviction to undertake the leadership role for establishing a more equitable, diverse, and just community.

Edgardo has a unique ability to make us all recall our ethnic roots and celebrate them. He has helped the community welcome the newcomers and enjoy and appreciate the richness they bring to our city.

Roland R. Blahnik, President & CEO, Goodwill Industries of Kentucky, 2006

Leadership in the social sector has no more powerful force than that leader who can combine vision with top management abilities to insure that he not only inspires, but knows how to guide the organization toward real, tangible results.

An organization with an eighty year history of service to the community, Goodwill Industries of Kentucky provides employment and training to disabled and disadvantaged Kentuckians, creating lasting change through the power of work. Each year hundreds of Kentuckians turn to Goodwill for a second chance at life, and to help them restore their families, build pride, and self respect.

When the current president and CEO, Roland R. Blahnik, arrived in 1984, Goodwill's prospects were bleak. They had just laid-off 130 workers and needed a loan to make payroll for the 23 remaining employees. Despite those challenges, Roland spoke clearly about a far-reaching vision for a future made brighter for those it serves, educates, and employs.

While Roland's bold vision seemed, at the time, improbable to many, Goodwill has witnessed a 22 percent annual growth and a 24 percent annual increase in mission wages to nearly $10,000,000 during the past two decades under his leadership. The number of employees has increased from 23 to more than 900, 77 percent of whom are disabled or disadvantaged. The past five years have been crucial, with the opening of nearly twenty new employment and training centers that employ hundreds of individuals who are disabled and disadvantaged. In 2006, Kentucky's Goodwill created 381 new jobs and set an organizational record, paying more than $10,000,000 in wages to the disabled and disadvantaged. Goodwill also initiated and successfully completed a fundraising campaign of $9,200,000—the largest in Goodwill's history.

As another indicator of this leadership success, the Kentucky office was recognized in this year as being one of the top ten most efficient Goodwill's in the nation as well as the eighteenth largest.

Kathy Beam, Head of School, Meredith Dunn, 2007

Leaders know what's important and how to keep everyone aligned on the important issues. Since becoming Head of School of Meredith Dunn in 2002, Kathy Beam has the led the school to become one of the most valuable community resources for children of all ages. Her leadership resulted in new and exciting curriculum enhancements, consistently high faculty and staff morale, and an energized board of directors.

Meredith Dunn School provides specialized instruction to children with a variety of learning disorders in grades 1st-8th. Faculty and staff understand that a child who has specific learning issues may become easily frustrated in a regular classroom setting. Within the school schedule, there is flexibility to address individual strengths and weaknesses and to optimize individual creativity.

Some of Kathy's specific accomplishments included doubling the professional development budget; adding art, music and drama to the curriculum; establishing a school-wide technology system; and increasing the amount of financial aid available to each student. In addition, she formed a partnership with Blue Apple Players to provide an artist in residence program for all grade levels which improves student visualization, reading comprehension, and auditory memory.

Kathy continually recruited and retained high caliber faculty and staff members, expanded outreach programs in the community, and balanced the school's limited finances while never compromising education programs or teacher/student ratios. In 2003, she adopted the nationally recognized Peace Builders Program which is a researched-based behavior program, with the tenets and language of the program being integrated throughout the total curriculum, supporting a school culture of respect, tolerance and accountability. In 2006, Meredith Dunn was named a model Peace Builder site.

Kathy's steady and enthusiastic, committed leadership are the catalyst behind the school's successes and its longer term vision.

Gordon Brown, President/CEO, Home of the Innocents, 2008

As any biographer of Lincoln will tell you, superior leadership is often a product of being able to engage others in the power of a good story. Gordon convinces other to follow through his use of stories. He engages people and rallies them to support the plight of abused, abandoned, and neglected children. He lives daily the belief that the Home should be our community's open arms to kids in crisis. He speaks with equal authenticity, passion, and advocacy about the Home to successful bankers, business leaders, legislators, line workers, and just about anyone who will listen.

In 2008, after a 17-year tenure at the helm, Gordon had led the Home through incredible growth and change as a result of his leadership. In just seven years not only had a new, state-of-the-art children's village been created and funded by $55 million in campaign gifts, but also thousands of children and their families have received care. Although many volunteers have helped in that process, Gordon has clearly been the primary leader and visionary and driving force behind these achievements.

Gordon has been the primary catalyst for challenging the 32-member board through a visionary strategic positioning process. After identifying critical planning issues through stakeholder surveys, the board established "broad directional arrows" to guide the management team as they developed specific strategies and action plans to address critical issues. The end result is a plan that has kept The Home strategically positioned to be more responsive to the ever changing external and internal environments while seeking to achieve its mission and vision in ways that best serve children and families.

Gordon's ability to lead and rally people to the support of children was dramatically illustrated as he led the campaign to build the Home's children's village, and again, to build five more desperately needed buildings. In both campaigns, his leadership resulted in multiple partners coming together to make these dreams a reality. Gordon was able to create a vision and then engage staff, board, volunteers, government (at federal, state, and local levels), local businesses, foundations, and countless individuals from throughout the community in working for and supporting these noble initiatives that helped advance the agency's mission and values.

Ramona Johnson, President & CEO, Bridgehaven, Inc., 2009

The human side of leadership is often expressed in its compassion, empathy, and willingness to roll up its sleeves and get the job done. Ramona Johnson has spent her 33-year career as a psychiatric nurse demonstrating profound respect for, and instilling hope in, people who suffer from mental illnesses. She has become highly skilled at providing compassionate and professional support both directly to clients and to the staff who serve them.

In her role as president and CEO, she must see to it that Bridgehaven provides the highest quality community-based rehabilitation and recovery services for adults with severe and persistent mental illness.

During her tenure in this leadership position, she has had to fight the endless battle for funding as traditional sources of money have either stagnated or receded. In her determined and continued dialogue with state officials, her efforts have yielded success, but the struggle must endure as she rallies her board and others to become forceful advocates for funding.

Ramona has demonstrated remarkable leadership while at Bridgehaven, directing a major shift in programming, from a medical model of treatment to a more recovery-oriented and client-empowered model of psychiatric rehabilitation—in keeping with evolving best-practice standards in the field. This transition was a three-year training process and included an intense multidisciplinary approach. Ramona's "in the trenches with you" approach, along with her sense of humor, cheerleading, and flexibility to alter plans to take into account changing circumstances, is a superb example of strong leadership.

Craig Buthod, Library Director, Louisville Free Public Library, 2010

Adversity in command can yield the best aspects of one's leadership capacity. Leaders know how to make lemonade when circumstances hand you nothing but lemons.

Consider the challenges of having the leadership responsibilities of the Louisville Free Public Library (LFPL). Aside from the extensive resource management of properties and facilities, you are charged with the mission to provide the people of Louisville with the broadest possible access to knowledge, ideas and information and to support them in their pursuit of learning. You serve a public of nearly half-million card holders and 3.5 million 'door-count' visitors annually.

Craig Buthod has been at the LFPL's leadership helm for the past twelve years. Facing dwindling budgets and staff cuts, he has nonetheless managed to strengthen every area of programming and services, including the library's collections, enhancing technology (especially in the area of public access to computers and specialized databases), and tenaciously pursuing the implementation of the library's Master Facilities Plan.

The library has continued in its successful support of literacy through activities such as the Summer Reading program, education through its GED curriculum, programs for new immigrants, author appearances, and technology classes.

Craig has steered his organization's efforts in direct support of the community's youth reading proficiency goals and toward an enhanced, better-educated workforce. He has built solid relationships with the Library's Foundation donor base, growing its confidence and contributions from $297,000 annually when he first arrived to over $1,000,000 in 2009.

In the midst of all these accomplishments, in August 2009, Craig had to guide the main branch of the library through the devastating effects of a sudden major flood that filled the basement in minutes, submerging the Library's operations, IT department, collection development, facilities management, book sorting, and delivery services. A wholesale replacement of this massive part of the library's infrastructure had to be initiated. Craig successfully led this effort bringing about restoration of this critical main branch in an astonishingly brief time.

For this heroic effort as well as his continued numerous successes in mission fulfillment over the past twelve years, Craig's leadership was recognized nationally by the *Library Journal*'s award of Librarian of the Year.

Section III

Spotlight on: Art of Leadership: Lynnie Meyer, 2002

Successful leaders communicate well. Leaders are gifted listeners. Leaders clearly characterize the reality of their organization's current and future situation. Leaders model the way through demonstrating that they are willing to bear the same burdens that they ask of those they lead.

While all of the Pyramid award winners in this category possess many or all of these attributes, the 2002 Pyramid Award winner in the Leadership category, Lynnie Meyer, is a riveting example of an energizing force that takes an organization to dizzying new heights of mission success.

When Lynnie became executive director of the Center for Women and Families in April of 1998, she came to the position with a nursing background, but no particular expertise in social work. However, she was well schooled in nursing disciplines of assessment, planning, reevaluating, and reacting. She had studied and was devoted to the principles of process improvement and quality management. To bring herself up to speed with the primary issues at the Center, she started her first big task: listening.

"I interviewed all the staff. I questioned every member of the board. I interviewed our top thirty donors. In every case I kept asking, 'What would it take to make the Center successful? What would you do if you were in my position?' I questioned and listened for the first 60 days I was on the job," she explained.

Lynne then applied the wisdom of Shunryu Suzuki's writing in his work *Zen Mind, Beginner's Mind*, "In the beginner's mind there are many possibilities; in the expert's there are few." Lynnie began to understand and act upon the underlying forces that kept the Center's stakeholders imprisoned in their situation of family violence: lack of education, housing, transportation, and child care. She began the process of developing programmatic answers to address these issues that went well beyond the basic temporary sheltering benefit the Center historically provided.

She relentlessly drove the development of these activities, not just awaiting the funding, but investing her faith in this compelling new approach. "I believe that if you cast the vision, the money will follow," she recounted. "And that happened in every one of these cases." Her convincing vision of what the Center could offer in new ways of helping people persuaded donors to underwrite the efforts. The Center began offering integrated on-site services for domestic assault victims, including total assessment of their participants' needs, on-site medical and legal help, all of which made the healing and recovery process so much more efficient and comforting to those who sought their aid. The Center began offering classes toward GED certification to address women's education needs, and providing resources in child care. In acknowledging the wider need for these services under her leadership, she spearheaded the campaign to extend the reach of the Center into Southern Indiana as well.

Lynnie's leadership style and charismatic presence are defined by her intense laser-like focus on mission, planning and, most importantly, results. She instilled into her management team a profound appreciation of proper execution of plans, their obligation to total accountability, teaching them to remain steadily focused on outcomes and how they tied back to mission success.

She then actively enlisted broad community support through her demonstration of the Center's evolving success and its deep devotion to its vision. She articulated the need so well that the she enlarged the "tent" of political and financial support that gathered to embrace the Center's mission throughout the community.

As part of her legacy, Lynnie's eight-year leadership left not only the Center at a higher level of mission effectiveness, changing countless lives, but also in the culture of new leadership that she engendered in the staff. Many of those who served under her leadership have gone into successful leadership roles in the Louisville regional social sector, no doubt having learned much by serving under Lynnie's command.

THE ART OF GOVERNANCE

CHAPTER 3

"The buck stops here."
—SIGN ON PRESIDENT HARRY TRUMAN'S OVAL OFFICE DESK

A truly effective, conscientious governing board makes all the difference in bringing about mission success. This is how it should be, given the fact that the social sector organization's board of directors has the authority and ultimate responsibility for its performance. This assertion may strike a discordant note with people who have witnessed social sector groups that have attained astonishing successes without— or more to the point—in spite of, the board of directors. But academic research continues to point toward a very strong correlation between boards that govern well and those social profit organizations that they oversee making significant strides in mission success.

Boards struggle over the concept of governance; most board members are well intentioned, but often misunderstand the meaning and demands of good responsible governance. Most simply assume that the term is "governance" nothing more than a fancy synonym for "management." Still other board members, very familiar with the models of for-profit boards based on their professional experience, have a clearer concept of governing principles, but don't grasp the wide points of divergence between the for-profit and social sector board responsibilities.

Three Covenants

Successful social profit sector governance demands a covenant relationship to be established and nurtured between the members of the board and three other entities: the mission, the community, and each other. It's more than a mere promise. Covenant in this sense invokes the depth of sincerity and sense of endlessness in its binding commitment.

A social sector board, when it actualizes its governing role, assures each of its partners of these intentions:

- To the Mission: we will provide conscientious oversight to the operations, insure that resources will be provided, guard its commitment to integrity, and while staying faithful to the values, strategically guide the organization steadily toward its vision.
- To the Community: we will act as faithful stewards of the resources, maintain transparency in reporting responsibly about the stewardship of resources, and adapt to community needs.
- To Each Other: we will support one another in our common tasks, build a culture of teamwork and collegiality, and hold one another accountable for our success.

Covenant with the Mission

In the social sector realm everything revolves around the mission. All strategies, all programs, all resources, and all decisions have to be considered in terms of their relationship to mission success. Of the many activities the board must focus upon with regard to the mission, none are more important than to insure its clarity and the sure, demonstrable movement towards its achievement.

The governing board has an obligation to elicit support for this mission in a number of ways: as evangelists of the mission, as resource providers, and guarantors of the organization's faithfulness to its values and integrity.

Evangelist Role

No one should take on the responsibility of becoming a social profit board member without possessing a passion for the vision and an unyielding faith in the mission. Adapting to that role, board members should commit to both formal and informal ways of expressing their enthusiasm and support by talking to their friends, colleagues, and anyone else they could influence about the importance of this work, and why they feel so ardent about the need for this mission to be successful. They should be prepared to express their enthusiasm, supported by evidence of the basic community need that is being resolved by the mission, and the social profit's success so far in pursuit of it.

For example, consider a social sector organization whose mission is to reverse the devastating trend of childhood obesity in a community through educating parents and children on the benefits of healthy eating and physical exercise. Board members could equip themselves with a series of talking points, the typical thirty-second "elevator speech" that they could use in promoting the essential ideas about how obesity in on the rise, the damage it means to our children, and how to reverse this dreadful trend. Even more, the board could also prepare (or ask the staff to prepare) a semi-formal presentation to be easily used by any board member who volunteers to take the mission/message to his next appearance at a Rotary Club, for instance.

Another board role in promulgating the mission might be through writing letters to the local newspaper editor, once again, to speak out about the obesity trend, promote the organization's activities to fight for children's health, or promote other ways in which their group could offer hope to those who were seeking help with this community medical threat.

Resource Providers

If acting like roving ambassadors sounds like behavior that will eventually include asking for donations of time and money, of course, it is the next logical step. There's no truer evidence of a board member's dedication to the mission than in actively engaging in resource development.

No accountable governing board can absolve itself of ducking this responsibility. No matter how large or sophisticated the social sector organization, no matter how large the professional fundraising staff that may be employed, none of those factors impact the essential truth of the board commitment: if you believe in the mission and publicly demonstrate this by joining the board, you must participate in some tangible way to bring in resources.

A board member's personal monetary commitment is always the first and most evident example of this support. Any board member who makes a decision to refrain from making any such financial contribution, is in effect, making this statement: "I believe deeply in this organization and hold its mission success as paramount, but I personally won't give it one thin dime of my own support." The dissonance of these two opposing stands is staggering. It is reminiscent of the renowned Groucho Marx line "I don't want to belong to any club that will accept me as a member."

Beyond the issue of personal contributions is the even more sensitive notion about the board's role in raising money. For a start-up social profit organization, this isn't an issue—if the board doesn't actively seek funds for the fledgling organization, the organization will quickly wither and fade away. The more important issue revolves around the more mature organization, one that has survived into adolescence or beyond, and has staff support that might have assumed a significant role in the fund development process. Even with those resources, the overwhelming logic of board primacy in ultimately owning responsibility for an organization's success means the board cannot exempt itself from this vital fund development role.

Every board has the freedom to create and craft the ways in which the board can engage itself in soliciting funds. It can range from asking board members to target and seek potential donors, to asking board members to become actively involved in helping build the booths for the annual fundraising event; it can include such activities as having board member write or call donors to thank them personally for their contributions; it can be as inventive as having board members canvass local retailers for silent auction items or officiating and handing out water bottles at the annual fundraising walk-a-thon. The fundamental principles to apply are these: every board member should select, commit to, and perform the fundraising activity that she's most comfortable with in pursuit of bringing in financial support.

Guarantors of Integrity

The final point of the mission covenant contains commitment aligning values and behaviors. Key among these is the pledge that all board members implicitly make upon joining a board that every decision represents the best interest of the organization. Individual board member interests, especially ones that might offer real or perceived notions of personal benefit, have no merit and are never acceptable. Responsible boards enforce conflict of interest policies to insure the board understands and stays in compliance with these principles.

The integrity issue embraces other aspects of the culture the board wants to create throughout the organization. Best expressed in the form of a written set of value commitments, the most effective ones typically preface each value with phrases such as "We believe . . ." and "We promise . . ."

Going back to the example of the childhood obesity group, their value charter might contain statements such as: "We believe: (1) that sound nutrition is the right of every child in our community; (2) that the introduction of "industrial foods" (e.g., loaded with high sugar, fat, and salt and low nutritional content) leads to obesity; (3) that children and families deserve to understand the consequences of their food choices; (4) We promise to educate the community about these hazards, etc... ."

These statements offer the board and staff the principle touchstones that guide strategic and tactical decision-making. Having these principles in mind will not only lead to smart program activities, but will also keep the organization on course for other decisions as well. For example, imagine the contradiction that would arise if the obesity-fighting organization were to sponsor a 5k fundraising walk and offer gift certificates to McDonalds as incentives for children to participate. This would represent a major disjoint between the spirit of the mission and those rewards, sending very confusing messages to the children, community, and donors. The unintended hypocrisy invites embarrassment and a tremendous loss of public respect. This kind of damage can be completely avoided if the board has—and lives—in constant harmony with its abiding values.

Covenant with the Community

All social sector boards must act as guarantors to the mission's "stakeholders" who essentially are the primary beneficiaries of the services. Peter Drucker, one the preeminent business sages in both the for-profit and social sectors in the twentieth century, always offered the insight that social sector boards need absolute clarity about who's being served by the mission and understanding their continuing (and changing) needs. After all, it's impossible to establish a covenant if you don't know the contracted party with whom it is established, or can't grasp their requirements.

The ultimate aspects of the community-focused covenant that are inherent in social sector board service are composed of these three characteristics: continuing awareness of the issues, faithful stewardship over the resources, and strategic leadership toward mission success.

Awareness of the Issues

Oversight of any social sector organization demands a fundamental grasp of the community issues in which the mission takes place. No governing board can claim to be responsibly governing without some foundational grasp of the very meaning of and dynamics that surround the core mission. Return again to the childhood obesity example: its governing board should not be *completely* comprised of physicians and nutritionists, but wouldn't the conscious inclusion of one of each improve the board's effectiveness so they could educate the rest of the board on obesity issues? Similarly, it might serve the board well if someone has had personal experience with obesity or the related health issues that it causes to add to the board's perspective.

Beyond the wise choice of these kinds of experts, the board should use all available data sources, from staff, from community experts, and from general research to stay conversant with the broad national and local trends that add to the understanding of the problem and new evolving solutions. An informed board can use its awareness as a filter when considering proposals that may come from the programming staff. The value of the board greatly increases when it engages in respectful dialogue over major operational proposals. A board that keeps itself perpetually in the dark around the needs and nuances of the mission can easily allow itself to become too influenced by fads.

Stewardship of Resources

All social sector boards commit to an inherent fiduciary pledge to the community that says: we will insure that the resources provided to this organization will never be subjected to abuse or misuse. In other words, the board will insure that sound policies and procedures are in place so that resources are protected from theft or fraud. The board acts as the second set of eyes and ears to insure fiscal safeguards are in place, reviews program effectiveness, and insists upon sound risk management practices.

Back in 1980s when the breakthrough talks occurred on nuclear disarmament between the United States and the Soviet Union, President Reagan's phrase "trust, but verify" became part of the strategic dialogue. It's in this same spirit that a social profit board engages in its fiduciary oversight. Boards should implicitly trust that the executive director and staff are honorable; the act of oversight simply removes all doubt of any exceptions.

The struggle to increase resources in the social sector never ends. In the difficult financial times since the advent of the Great Recession in 2008, this burden has only become more onerous. The scarcity of financial resources has made it even more imperative to insure that these resources are never subjected to theft or embezzlement. The board therefore, has to establish policy and procedural safeguards to make such illegal acts impossible.

Using standard accounting controls and processes, many of which are well institutionalized and proven in the for-profit field, can offer a solid foundation of that guarantee. Boards need their own expertise, often in the form of a board member with an accounting background and knowledge of these principles to help insure compliance.

Beyond the very question of legitimate use of funds and approving budgets, boards also have to preside over the effective and efficient use of those funds in the social sector organization's program arena. The endless question in this part of governance comes from dwelling in this essential governance question: Is this organization really making any difference?

Returning to the childhood obesity organization example, the board should periodically review the essential outcomes of the major programs. For instance, this board would take Program A, the one that teaches parents about healthy food choices, and insist on seeing evidence over whether those classes are making a difference in parental purchasing behavior, children's eating behaviors, and ultimately—one would hope—improved children's health. Just looking at cursory program data, such as class attendance numbers does not tell the board about ultimate results.

This quest naturally requires a considerable amount of data gathering and administrative time on the part of the staff, but the oversight demands of the board and its accountability to the public and the donors is always the most important consideration. If a social sector organization finds, at the end of the day, that it has become ineffective in pursuit of its mission it must commit itself to reforming its programs.

The final facet of stewardship of resources falls within the realm of risk management practices that the social sector organization should employ. In this arena, the point is to minimize the chance of harm to any resources, especially people. Having general liability insurance in place is an obvious example. But there are more important aspects.

For example, our case-in-point childhood obesity organization may have a program that offers an exercise camp for children so they may learn healthy ways to engage in physical activities to help control their weight and improve their general health. Suppose the camp is staffed by a group of volunteer fitness experts. Because they are going to be in contact with young children—a recognized vulnerable population—a board with prudent risk management oversight would insist that background checks be conducted on all those volunteers to insure no one with any history of harming children would be recruited.

Successful governing boards know the difference between governance and management and stake the clear demarcation lines between themselves, the executive director, and the staff. They recognize that their job is in setting strategic direction, defining the broad general policy guidelines, and enlisting the public resources that give the management team the autonomy in which to enact the strategic intent of the board.

Boards with this kind of awareness empower the executive director with the authority and responsibility to execute the strategic plan without meddling into her management processes. Given this freedom to act, the executive director is still held closely accountable for successful operational command by the board through the use of agreed-upon tangible metrics.

Strategic Leadership

In an eighteenth century church in Sussex, England, stands a plaque that reads:

> "A vision without a task is but a dream; a task without a vision is drudgery; a vision and a task is the hope of the world."

The board's responsibility of bringing about the organizational vision as described in Chapter One can only be realized by the board's promise to orchestrate the periodic development of a broad strategic plan. Visions can only come into realization when people take action. Otherwise, visions turn out to be mirages.

To move the organization to its "promised land" or vision, the board must develop a strategic map providing the outline of the direction and pace at which the social profit must move to bring the ultimate dream into reality. The normal planning horizon of three-five years should describe the strategic needs in the community, the consequential major operations that will be undertaken to address them, and how those activities will be sustained financially. The strategy would also address other attendant resource areas such as staff, volunteers, marketing, technology, physical plant, including the board itself, and how each of those components must be adapted to advance the strategy.

No board should ever attempt to accomplish such an ambitious task alone. It needs the collegial input of staff, key donors, stakeholders, volunteers, and interested community representatives. Armed with these perspectives, the board has a better than even chance of assembling a reality-based assessment of the current health of the social profit organization, grounded on a solid sense of the critical environmental factors with which it must contend in the strategic future.

In their strategic planning mode, boards have to reconnect with their mission and vision. Contained within those documents are the abiding reminders of the social profit's ultimate destination, the North Star that guides all strategic decisions. Without the deep reflection and reminder of those concepts, strategies can become profoundly misguided.

The resultant strategic plan becomes the board's template for oversight of its operational progress. And there will be times where the plan will have to be strategically altered. For example, no one was sitting around the strategic planning table in 2007 said, "Let's also be prepared for the Great Recession is scheduled to arrive in the first quarter of 2008." But those who did have a plan had something from which they could re-adjust their goals to deal with the Great Recession.

Without a strategic map, no board can hope to offer any guidance other than to react to the abrupt buffeting of seemingly random events. Without a map, the seeming chaos of history will only invite a feeling of existential despair.

Covenant with One Another

The final covenant: Each board member must pledge to work

in solidarity with the rest of the board. This is the pledge that is least understood and least practiced. Yet, without this covenant, none of the other commitments to community or to mission can possibly succeed.

Boards as Teams

Good governance represents a thin veneer of behaviors that coats a core set of group behaviors simply called teamwork. If a board can't cohere as a team and apply the basic principles of teamwork, there's little chance of any effective governance.

The first unifying aspect of teams can be found in their common goal. With social sector boards this principle unmistakably restates the need for a commonly held, visibly stated vision and mission. Being invited to join a board implies that the new participant has a clear commitment to the vision and pledges to work with the others to bring it into reality.

While that unity is paramount, team members themselves are often selected based on the complementary skills or knowledge they possess. Football teams can't perform with eleven quarterbacks anymore than a basketball team made up entirely of forwards. Similarly, boards look to empanel their available positions with targeted diverse gifts of knowledge, skill, experience, background, expertise, or influence. Each board member should have an expressed special, significant attribute that is distinct and promise to use that talent to add to the team's overall performance capacity.

High performing teams hold one another accountable and at the same time work collegially to insure one another's (and therefore the entire group's) success. Specific responsibilities should be clear to each board member to guarantee that the group will succeed. People have to know what the board's rules are regarding meeting attendance, committee participation, donations, and the overall expected level of time involvement required to perform as a responsible board member. All of these details should be specifically spelled out in the board orientation materials.

A key interpersonal component that must be present in every effective team is trust. Trust comes in three significant dimensions as

Dennis and Michelle Reina explain in their work, *Trust and Betrayal in the Workplace*. People need to be trusted and respected in the competencies they bring to the team; they need to be trusted in their communications with the team (tell the truth, speak authentically); and finally, trusted in their contractual work (act dependably—do what's expected). Any board that can actively foster these behaviors rides along the royal road to high performing governance.

No team can function without some form of leadership, and that crucial role in governing boards properly belongs to the board chair. Beyond the normal ceremonial aspects of presiding at board meetings, competent board chairs act as coaches and cheerleaders to encourage the needed board member behaviors. The board chair should be quick to thank and reluctant to criticize, but still not tolerate behaviors such as cynicism, inattention to promised deadlines, unexplained absenteeism, or any violation of ethics or contradictions to the values proclaimed by the organization.

Boards, as is true with all teams, constantly change, with the resignation of veterans and the induction of new members. In order to preserve the integrity of a high functioning board, careful attention should be paid to the recruitment and socialization of new members. Recruitment requires a coherent set of standards that describes the essential characteristics that new candidates should possess, such as an abiding passion for the mission, a willingness to loyally support the organization through participation on the board, and financial support and careful devotion to understanding and resolving strategic matters that face the organization.

In addition, the board should look for secondary characteristics, ones that not every board must have, but that every board should have in order to round out the needed talent to govern well as a whole. So a board will recruit some aspects of talent in areas such as accounting, law, investment, strategic business management, and any other area that might contribute to the board's overall conceptual grasp of the issues regarding mission (e.g., a physician on the board of a health-related mission, or a choreographer on the board of a ballet theater).

Socialization means bringing the new board member up to speed with the organization—its history, the fundamental aspects of its resources, programs, operations and general fiscal health—as well as introducing the recruited person to the rest of the board. The most effective means of making this happen effectively and efficiently is through assigning the new board member a mentor—a veteran board member who can act as a trusted advisor, coach, and confidante.

The mentor can fill in the many gaps of information, things that are never explicitly covered in a typical board orientation document, especially around the areas of board members' personalities, information on sensitive issues over which different factions of the board struggle, and other aspects about the board's culture. The mentor can also ease the new board inductee's introduction into board committees to which he has been assigned.

CNPE's Governance Award Concepts

Comedian and author Woody Allen once said that, "Eighty percent of success is showing up." Boards of directors' success starts with this very important truth: the highly effective governing board has high rates of attendance and engagement at all board meetings. There's never any issue around having a quorum in order to conduct business. In fact, the full talent of the board routinely makes itself present so that the full discussion and deliberations of the governing issues have the benefit of all their wise counsel.

Additionally, this kind of board has joined into a true partnership, supporting the mission, the community and one another by actively volunteering to serve on well-functioning committees, never at a want for board members showing up at fundraising events, speaking at public forums to advocate for the mission, or opening doors to influential potential donors in order to have a discussion about financial support.

These boards have yet another important dimension beyond just having members faithfully present in the board sessions. They also do real governance work. They periodically review the programs to insure that they are having a mission effect and demand changes if they're not providing valid outcomes. They scrupulously oversee the financials, applying the appropriate analysis to assure the organization's sustainability, as well as gaining the assurance that resources are being expended in accordance with their policy guidelines.

Section II

ART OF GOVERNANCE AWARD WINNERS

Louisville Metro United Way Board of Directors, 2001

One of the most fundamental aspects of governance emanates from the board's enduring dedication to the strategic positioning of the agency.

Metro United Way (MUW) is the area's largest private funder of health and human service agencies that serves the eight counties of Jefferson, Hardin, Oldham, Shelby and Bullitt counties in Kentucky and Clark, Floyd and Harrison counties in southern Indiana.

Metro United Way has extensive community involvement within its committee structure, community investment teams, and board of directors. Despite these complex factors, MUW's governance displays clear and compelling evidence that its structure and volunteer talent serve the community extremely well.

The vibrant direction that emerged from the board's oversight of their strategic plan, known as Vision 2010, promised to maximize the contributions it raises and allocates through Metro United Way's leadership and coordination. During the period of 2000-2001, staff and volunteers identified more than 60 short- and long-range priorities they deemed as crucial to creating the community that is mapped in Vision 2010. After an active discussion of potential priorities, the board selected the top 20 priorities for 2001 and 2002.

Through this governance structure and process, Metro United Way's board of directors has championed a dialogue among numerous constituents in the community around what it takes for agencies to work together effectively. It has demonstrated the high level of stewardship and accountability that is essential to protect and nurture the trust that forms the heart of the donor-partner relationship.

By embracing community involvement, generating a common vision, involving the whole of the organization, identifying strategies to reach goals, and connecting the annual plan to the overall plan with budgeted resources, Metro United Way's board of directors has provided a model of excellence in collective governance.

Home of the Innocence Board of Directors, 2002
(See Spotlight, Section III, p. 59)

Brooklawn Board of Directors, 2003

Governing boards can be the primary agent for significant turnarounds in social profits' history. They can reset the proper strategic direction and insure that resources will be made available to sustain that renaissance. Brooklawn's board provides an example.

Brooklawn provides comprehensive care, treatment, and education to emotionally and behaviorally troubled children and teens and to their family (or foster family). Children are referred to Brooklawn from the state Cabinet for Families and Children, psychiatric hospitals, private practitioners, and families themselves.

In the early 1990, Brooklawn faced imminent danger of closing its doors for good after Kentucky Medicaid had decided to cut off reimbursements for the programs Brooklawn sponsored at that time. The board considered merger or disbanding Brooklawn. Instead, the board realized the gap that would be created in the community for children who needed this kind of care. The board decided to march ahead, taking Brooklawn boldly into a new era of service, as a residential treatment resource for children with serious emotional disturbances. In taking this initiative, Brooklawn took its first step toward becoming a pioneer in successful residential mental health services for teens.

Through its careful selection of a new executive director, David Graves, and its building a new and ambitious long-term strategy, the board led the way in securing new and abundant funding streams that provided new capacity for Brooklawn's operational needs. Through the board's wise oversight and David Graves' gifted execution of the strategic plan, Brooklawn's reputation for quality results and reputation for excellence in its program outcomes became well known. The state agency, then called the Cabinet for Families and Children, produced reports demonstrating how Brooklawn had become one of the most cost-efficient providers in the region. The feedback from clients and families reflected their high levels of satisfaction with Brooklawn's care and treatment programs.

Beyond its own mission impact, Brooklawn went on to become an active leader among the Metro United Way agencies and worked in partnership with the University of Louisville and Spalding University to provide training for graduate students in three different programs. Brooklawn went on to be an active member in statewide Children's Alliance and the Kentucky Mental Health Coalition. In the space of a decade, under the careful guidance of a responsible board, Brooklawn had become totally transformed.

Actors Theater of Louisville Board of Directors, 2004

(See Spotlight, Section III, p. 62)

River City Housing Board of Directors, 2005

Many boards function best in a "hands-on" mode, especially in the early stages of a social profit's existence when there are little or no staff resources to perform the on-the-ground operations. River City's Housing board, aside from its normal governance role, was an activist board as well.

River City Housing (RCH) is a social profit housing developer whose mission is to increase the availability of safe, decent, affordable housing for low-income first-time home buyers. The board of directors has encouraged and made possible a level of productivity and growth in development that would have otherwise been impossible for an organization that operated, until 2004, with only one full-time staff member.

RCH began in the mid 1990s as a program led by three community ministries and originally confined its reach to three service areas in eastern sections of Louisville. Seeing additional need and equipped with the support of a great board, it has expanded its service territory county wide.

By 2005, RCH had become one of approximately ten Community Development Housing Organizations (CHDO) in Metro Louisville. RCH became a significant contributor to this category of new home construction. Of seventeen CHDO homes built in Louisville in 2004, River City Housing built fourteen.

Thanks to the hands-on construction expertise of individual members, RCH in that same year joined with Louisville Metro government to build twelve new homes in West Louisville designated as replacement housing for the Clarksdale Housing development. This board worked together as a team, allowing each member to excel in areas of individual expertise. An individual board member was lead inspector for each house built.

The RCH Board continually revisits the mission of the organization, asking whether a project is central to its mission and not being afraid to decline an opportunity when it is not a good fit. The Board protects RCH resources by intelligently assessing risk, which can significantly impact the success of any housing development. In 2005, the board oversaw changes in the agency's accounting system to better evaluate financing strategies.

Big Brothers Big Sisters of Kentuckiana Board of Directors, 2006

Blending traditional oversight duties and demonstrating dedication to the mission by being actively engaged in critical mission-related programs is not strictly found just in start-up social profits. There are plenty of opportunities for boards of well-established social profits to proclaim their personal allegiance to the mission. Big Brothers Big Sisters of Kentuckiana's board won based on these hallmarks of good governance.

Big Brothers Big Sisters of America has been a congressionally chartered social profit federation for over 100 years. Big Brothers Big Sisters provides one-to-one mentoring services for children of untapped potential in the United States.

In 2005, the Big Brothers Big Sisters of Kentuckiana served at-risk children in twelve counties in Kentucky and Southern Indiana. Their community and school-based mentoring programs promote education, self-esteem, and healthy lifestyles and relationships.

The board's structure and leadership has been revamped in an innovative way. The number of committees was reduced to just three committees, now focused in highly targeted areas. With an eye on overall vision and strategy, the newly restructured board helped the organization set and mobilize to achieve key performance milestones. Big Brothers Big Sisters experienced a $60,000 increase in pledges through the restructured "Bowl for Kids Sake" program. From 2003-2006, the organization has increased the number of children served in one-to-one matches by 50 percent. An inspiring facet of the Big Brothers Big Sisters board is that many of them serve as mentors as well. At each board meeting, the members discuss an experience working as a mentor, bringing the focus clearly onto the activities of the organization.

By 2006, Big Brothers Big Sisters of Kentuckiana had become one of the top 15 quality agencies out of the 500 Big Brothers Big Sisters organizations in the nation.

Brightside Inc. Board of Directors, 2007

As part of any strategic plan, boards often have to consider how the board itself is performing in its role of governance. This kind of self-reflection offers the chance of board renewal and resulting better leadership, which then brings higher mission success. This was Brightside's case in 2007.

Brightside, Inc. is a 501(c)(3) organization that operates as a public/private partnership with Metro Government. Services to Metro Louisville include landscaping, neighborhood clean-ups, and school programs. Its mission is to unite people in clean and green activities to beautify the city and foster pride in our community. By the end of 2007, over 10,000 citizens volunteered in Brightside's various beatification activities.

In 2006, the Brightside Board of Directors began a strategic planning process. The Board had always provided active oversight of mission and program outcomes. In its new strategic planning cycle, the board constructed a three-point plan to strengthen its governance of the organization. The board had decided to meet more frequently. The board revamped its crucial committee configuration to include financial, governance and strategic oversight committees. The board then recruited new members, adding new insight and energy to the group's governance culture.

As a result of these changes the board's governance work became much more effective. Board attendance increased and participation became stronger, and the board's ability to tackle tough governance issues was streamlined. The board also dramatically improved its capacity for fund development, producing a 20 percent increase in its fundraising outcomes compared to previous years.

The board also embraced the challenge of constructing a 10 year planning vision for Brightside that would provide overall planned growth and sustainability for Brightside's programming.

GuardiaCare Services, Inc. Board of Directors, 2008

"Engage, engage, engage," should be the mantra of every board member—to become active in every way possible to contribute the insight, skills, money, and any other personal "gift" of expertise toward mission success. GuardiaCare Services had this very experience with their board in 2008.

Since 2004, GuardiaCare Services has expanded their board of directors, adding greater diversity in age, ethnicity, and occupational knowledge. After completing a self-assessment of organizational and board effectiveness, GuardiaCare Services began updating its strategic plan and charting the course for the period 2009-2012.

The board had already succeeded in its quest to achieve 100 percent financial participation in the personal contributions from each board member. The board became active in securing new grants, launched a Capital Fund that addressed long-deferred improvements to the physical plant, and inaugurated several successful fundraising events, all of which have witnessed full board participation.

Beyond these laudable achievements, GuardiaCare Services has fully engaged individual members of the board to bring their specific skills, talents, connections, and relationships to bear on the organization's mission.

Some of these skills, talents and resources that have resulted in significant improvements include:
- New logo and marketing video
- Concept of *Secrets of Louisville Chefs Kitchen Theatre Gala*
- An arrangement with Kentuckiana Planning and Development Agency to conduct home safety assessments by licensed Occupational Therapists in homes of seniors
- Practices to engage legal counsel for clients
- Exceptional leadership on the board in telling the story of the power and value of mission

Board accomplishments are often celebrated in terms of their collective impact on the organization. A unique approach to the GuardiaCare Services Board is how much it has cultivated the talents and interest of each board member as it reaches for its vision, grounded by its mission.

Gilda's Club Board of Directors, 2009

Founding boards literally radiate the energy that emits from their deeply felt passion for the vision. They may not have many other resources at this starting stage, but determination and optimism provides the enduring strength to face and fight the considerable obstacles in their way.

For Gilda's Club, success built upon early success in this remarkable display of governance. Despite the fact that to be on this board, each director has to pledge an enormous amount of time and energy in supporting this mission, people are clamoring to be invited to serve.

The mission of the Louisville Chapter of Gilda's Club is to create a welcoming community of free support for everyone living with cancer—men, women, teens, and children—along with their families and friends. This innovative program is an essential complement to medical care, providing networking and support groups, workshops, education, and social activities.

From the outset, the founding board of Louisville's Gilda's Club agreed "to do it right, do it big, and do it with class." The advice from other Gilda's Clubs that had already been established in the US was to be realistic about fundraising—it would be a difficult challenge. They advised caution, advocating that they start small, minimize risk and expectations. Expect it to take five years or more to raise the $2-3 million for a proper facility. Be prepared, said the established clubs, for people to perceive it as a place for women cancer patients only, and not to expect much in terms of a diverse attendance: most participants will be white women.

Despite the cautionary warnings, the board plunged ahead into a $5.4 million capital campaign, pledging over $750,000 themselves with the plan to acquire a facility over twice the recommended initial square footage, and to own it free of debt. In addition, the board presided over the facility planning, building special meeting spaces for teens and children. They purposely devised programs to attract and invite the wide diversity of those affected by cancer so that Gilda's Club quickly became an oasis of support for children, teens, men, women, and all ethnicities.

The board and staff's outreach to physicians and hospitals and to the local coalition of hospices got the word out fast to the community: Gilda's Club was an inviting place, free to all who wanted to partake, that offered an atmosphere of caring support to all those affected by cancer.

The board continues its strategic outreach planning to increase

Gilda's collaboration with a host of other agencies—hospitals, cancer support groups, and medical research facilities—in the Louisville community to insure that everyone knows about Gilda's Club so it can serve the entire population.

Junior Achievement of Kentuckiana Board, 2010

Every governing board needs to find a way to insure that all of its participants are actively engaged in all aspects of governance. There are many potential paths to this goal, the most successful being the ones that offer a rich mix of ways to become engaged and a means to insure that the board holds itself accountable for good governance results.

Junior Achievement (JA) of Kentuckiana's mission is to inspire and prepare young people to succeed in the global economy.

JA of Kentuckiana's board has developed a team culture and framework to invite continued and varied means for board members to stay highly active. They've essentially transformed what many normally view as unenviable governing tasks into activities that are now seen as enjoyable under a structure of friendly, competitive and creative score keeping among competing board "teams."

Labeled "Board Olympics," the board team members now actively seek ways they can be more participative in order to earn "points" for their respective teams. This approach offers the board an inventive way to understand how they can be more productive. This method drives up the likelihood that board members will get to know one another better, fostering a greater sense of collegiality and shared responsibility. It transforms even the most routine acts of board governance into something experienced as exciting and rewarding.

As a consequence of using this reframing of board governance, there are no longer any 'under performing' problems among board members; there's no longer the worry of a developing gap between active and inactive board participants, and everyone feels a growing sense of becoming more actively involved in activities including fundraising, program management, volunteer recruitment, and proselytizing the good work of JA all over the community.

Section III

SPOTLIGHT ON: ART OF GOVERNANCE: HOME OF THE INNOCENTS, 2002

In 2002, CNPE's Art of Governance award was given to the Home of the Innocents' board of directors. Founded in 1880, The Home of the Innocents' mission is to reach out and advocate for children, youth, and their families, by providing care and shelter during critical times. In 2001, the Home of the Innocents served over 2,000 children who had been abandoned, abused, neglected, or who were medically fragile.

In 1998, the board recognized that a radical solution would be needed to solve the physical space demands that the Home's expanding programs produced. Knowing that finding a whole new locale was the only realistic strategic answer, the board began a comprehensive search for a new site. After months of investigation, the board concluded that the recently abandoned Bourbon Stock Yards would be a perfect fit for the long-term vision of services to children.

The board embraced an ambitious plan to finance this endeavor, carefully choosing the right people to staff the capital campaign committee to raise the necessary $25,000,000 to construct its envisioned "children's village" on this 20-acre site. The board itself secured and donated over $625,000 to fund Phase One of the village with the 2001 opening of the Cralle-Day House for pregnant, parenting, and non-parenting teenage girls. Because of the increased space and home-like atmosphere this program will better teach girls parenting and life skills.

Since that time, the board has provided broad general oversight for the continuing development of the remaining planned facilities including the Kosair Charities' Pediatric Convalescent Center, four crisis care cottages, and Children's Commons. The board's selection for that ambitious 20 acres of development where the historic Bourbon Stockyards once stood has also spurred other positive development initiatives in the Phoenix Hill, Irish Hill, and Butchertown area, enhancing the value of its own new property.

The dramatically enhanced space allowed the Home of the Innocents to meet the needs of its children better than ever since it provided a "home" rather than a facility. Thanks to the board's foresight, imagination, vision, and action in securing the funding to bring about this ambitious dream's realization, it demonstrated outstanding characteristics of governance.

In a conversation with Gordon Brown, President and CEO of Home of the Innocents, he pointed out several long-standing attributes of his board's governance culture that has led to these remarkable mission achievements.

Gordon cites his board's culture as a crucial component of this success: "Our board understands its governance role consists of strategic planning, policy development and establishing the overall budget. It then turns the management responsibility over to me and my team to implement."

The board knows and respects the boundary lines between board and staff functions and responsibilities. Board members work in close concert with staff members in joint committee mechanisms, but all other board-staff communication flows properly through Gordon as the "eye of the needle" as he calls it, so there's no opportunity for violating his clear unity of command over the staff.

In addition, the board has a deeply held tradition and faith in the strategic planning process. They recognize that the ultimate success in this process is not the ultimate plan itself, but in the continuing planning process. Although the board re-creates the strategy in a formal way every four years or so, it also tunes the plan on a continuing basis, adjusting it to seize upon new-found opportunities or steer clear of unanticipated threats. "Our board's faithfulness to strategic planning is an ultimate value," says Gordon

Home of the Innocents' Board has been able to develop and maintain these ideal governing behaviors over a number of years. By carefully knowing and vetting the type of person they would want to call to serve on the board, by using the committee structure as an apprenticeship "greenhouse," and finally by developing a comprehensive orientation and mentoring system, new board members are given a thorough grasp of the group behaviors that yield successful governance outcomes. They carefully groom many of their upcoming board candidates first through service on their committees in order to acclimatize them to Home of the Innocents' issues and values.

While they would gladly welcome anyone with a proven track record of management success, political influence, or personal wealth, they won't abide any breach of protocol in their governance culture. There's no room for outsized egos that would be tempted to hijack board priorities or disrupt the board's sense of shared power. The board maintains its tradition of close collegiality through forthright coaching of each new member about proper principles of governance behavior.

Spotlight on: Art of Governance: Actors Theater of Louisville, 2004

One of the enduring legendary artistic lights in the Louisville landscape over the last four decades has been Actors Theater of Louisville. A winner of a host of coveted awards and worldwide recognition for excellence, Actors has been a leader in the creation of new plays and in the re-creation of the classics. The organization's vision to build a home for inspirational collaboration that leads to creative excellence in American theater has driven its on-going success.

Governed by a professionally and culturally diverse board of some forty people back in 2004, the board displayed outstanding responsible governance behavior in many strategic ways.

It was during this era that the board had just completed a strategic plan, according to the then-executive/managing director, Alexander "Sandy" Speer, which focused upon the long-term sustainability of the theater. Working in close concert with staff, informed by community focus groups, and supported by detailed research involving earned revenue and theater capacity utilization, the board guided the organization toward an ambitious capital and endowment campaign of some $12 million. Then, in a true representation of their allegiance to the vision of Actors, 100 percent of the board pledged long-term support totaling $5.2 million of that campaign. Over the years, that strategic turning point has made a significant difference in insuring the theater's capacity to grow and its long-term sustainability.

The board has also maintained its vigilance in critical areas such as leadership transition. After the 31-year success of artistic director, Jon Jory, the board's deliberation and careful selection process brought about the successful era of the current artistic director, Marc Masterson. The board has similarly guided the leadership transition from the theater's managing director from Sandy Spear's forty-year tenure to handing that essential leadership responsibility to Jennifer Bielstein in 2006.

Jennifer commented that the theater enjoys to this day the long-term strategic foresight of its past governing boards' wise decisions. They made the strategic choice for example to place Actors in its prime Main Street locale, pioneering the eventual realization of the Main Street renaissance of business and artistic endeavors that grace that part of downtown Louisville. Those past boards have also made the very prescient real estate decisions in the neighboring area. These neighboring sites insure that the theater's capacity to house its artistic offerings, and to provide its crucial back-office administration and production facilities.

The board's focus also extends to production strategies as well. Jennifer offers that "In these economic times when support for the arts has particular vulnerability, the board continues to recognize and support our key integral strengths. They react to these times, not by cutting to the bone, but by galvanizing new resources to meet these challenges."

This enduring inheritance of highly committed, strategically driven boards has been one of Actors Theater's many advantages and offers an outstanding example of the long-term effects of responsible governance.

The Art of Collaboration

CHAPTER 4

"It is the long history of humankind (and animal kind, too) those who learned to collaborate and improvise most effectively have prevailed."
—**Charles Darwin**

Charles Darwin would be appalled to learn that he is continuously cited for a phrase he never authored: "survival of the fittest." His assertion was that survival is awarded to the most *adaptive*. Humans inherited both the innate capacity and the biological necessity to work with one another in order to survive. Whether in defending one another from the predations of a saber-tooth tiger or working as a team to take down a wooly mammoth for nourishment, our successful forbearers passed along the behavioral advantage of working together toward common goals. To this very day, humanity can only find its last true hope in confronting problems as a community. In the social sector, this work manifests itself in the formation of individual social profit organizations, and then, more significantly, in those organizations collaborating with one another on common interests.

Collaboration, as defined by different experts, has a number of attributes. Among the most critical are that it involves:

- Two or more organizations

- Mutual (but not necessarily the same) benefit for all agreed participants
- Detailed, well-defined structure on roles and responsibilities
- Joint accountability
- Defined structural responsibility
- Shared resources and authority

Collaboration differs significantly from two other lower-level commitment activities that sound synonymous—cooperation and coordination. Cooperation generally involves information sharing, but no sharing of authority and responsibility. Coordination takes the mutual involvement up a step higher. The focus on a specific activity in coordination does take a higher identity of risk and responsibility compared to cooperation. While coordination and cooperation are principally tactical measures, collaboration represents a strategic operation.

Collaboration moves the relationship between the members to a significantly more intense level of risk and resource engagement. Successful collaboration requires a higher degree of communication among the participating parties, as well as an advanced level of mutual trust. Learning to trust others in another organization to accomplish a task, thereby making oneself essentially dependent (vulnerable) on that relationship is something that cannot succeed without trusting that the other side has the competence and the honest commitment to the task.

Forming a collaborative effort takes an enormous amount of time to communicate, nurture relationships, and engage in detailed negotiations about roles, accountabilities, resource sharing, costs, and outcomes that will accrue to each participant. The potential rewards are high, but the risk side is steep with the huge expenditure of management time in negotiating and forging the working interactions. Why should any organization be compelled to distract itself from its normal independent work and take the collaborative road?

One of the biggest reasons in the social sector comes from the organizations that fund social profits. Grantors have long insisted that the growth of social profit organizations has gone out of control in the last twenty years. Estimates are that the number of registered social profits grew by 30 percent from 1997 to 2007. Recent national estimates are that 45,000 to 60,000 new social profits form every year in this nation. No reliable estimates exist on how many take root and survive past their first five years. The point is, according to funders, that the social profits bloom ungoverned all over the landscape, duplicate effort, don't interact with one another, confuse donors over which is best suited to accomplish a goal, and only increase the desperate competition for the dwindling donor resources. Funders are increasing their bias toward awarding grants to social profits whose programmatic efforts show a demonstrated willingness and experience with collaborating with other agencies.

The Great Recession in its punishing length and depth over the last 30 months, has reduced the flow of money to the social sector from all traditional sources—individual donors, foundations, and government—and pressured the social profits into considering collaborative efforts in order to reduce costs as one means of relief from the resulting resource drought.

Another variable that has fostered the development of collaboration has come from the increased complexity of the social issues that the sector addresses. Many social profits engaged in human services no longer exist simply to feed the hungry, shelter the homeless, and comfort the sick. They seek to treat the underlying aspects of those social concerns with the hope that if the causal social structures which lead to poverty, hunger, and illness, can be addressed—at both the community and individual level—then the-long term changes for the better will ultimately come about. This adds huge difficulty to the task. So, for example, a homeless shelter will not only look to provide temporary shelter, but look for ways to break the cycle and syndrome that leads to homelessness—a vastly more complicated task than simply maintaining beds in a comfortable building. Added, these layers of responsibility improve the likelihood that no one agency can amass the right resources to solve this issue. This requirement increases the logic of engaging other agencies that have the expertise and resources to help as well.

Collaborations are not restricted to simply interconnecting social profits by themselves. Many collaborative efforts can engage organizations from across the entire spectrum of a community, engaging government, for-profits, and social profits, each with its own particular strengths and interests and potential rewards. One can witness, for example, a collaborative effort for rehabilitating convicts, involving a state penal agency working with a social profit involved in giving that population temporary housing and workforce training, and a private enterprise financially underwriting that program so that the re-trained workers can be employed by that for-profit.

Compelling as collaboration can be, it doesn't come into being easily, especially if it is driven by adverse circumstances such as severe economic downturns. Many organizations that have had a successful track record in the past without collaboration, often regard this outreach as a signal of weakness or failure. The board of directors may be reluctant to assume the risks of such a strategic enterprise. The lack of experience and trust in working with other agencies can appear as an admission of failure, something no board wants to countenance. Finally, there exists the natural concern over leaving the boundaries of the comfortable, even if inadequate, confines of one's own group. "Hell," the French existentialist thinker Jean-Paul Sartre notably remarked, "is others."

To insure that an organization can build its capacity to collaborate a number of actions have to be taken. Research suggests that the most successful collaborative efforts evolve from a history of lesser involved activities such as cooperation and coordination. Collaborative groups have a culture that allows for seeing possibilities through interconnecting with outside resources. They see little value in the "lone wolf" approach, driven as they are by mission accomplishment by whatever means—including outreach.

Successful collaboration comes through a deep commitment to build trust and foster common interests. This requires the authentic leadership of the executive director as well as the board chair to explore and invite other organizations to common dialogue. They have to literally create a and maintain an on-going forum—the time, space, and energy to begin and continue the conversation. They may have to combat suspicion and work earnestly to show the potential collaborating agencies the higher vision of mutual benefit that they can all potentially achieve.

Successful collaboration cannot be achieved by simply connecting a leader-to-leader bond of trust. Presume for a moment that two board chairs of two different art museums in a state wanted to collaborate on hosting a major travelling exhibition of art. If the relationship and agreements begin to emerge without building similar trust and understanding with their respective museum directors and staff, this collaboration has little chance of success. The necessary commitment of time and level of detailed sharing of responsibilities won't develop unless every layer in both organizations connects with its counterpart in agreeing on sharing power, resources, commitments, and accountability.

In a very similar way, if collaborative efforts are forged just at the staff level without full strategic embrace and support of the board, collaboration can be fruitless. In collaborations, a well-functioning board can make use of a tremendous amount of its value through cutting red tape, summoning up resources from their organizations, or becoming very persuasive advocates in promoting these activities.

The final factor, then, indicates that collaborations take up a considerable amount of time at all of these levels. They have to be carefully planned, and mapped out, with appropriate time allotted to the participants, and budgets allocated to activities that surround all the behaviors leading up to and then executing the collaborative enterprise itself. The board will properly deploy its governance role through its strategic oversight—insuring that the collaborative effort is on track and that the forecasted mission benefits are in evidence—as well as behaving in ways to foster the collaborative initiative with other external organizations.

Over time, the social profits that build their capacity to be collaborative in order to advance mission will survive the Great Recession and thrive when the economy recovers. Those who cannot or will not embrace this behavior may become victims of the harsh social and economic atmospherics, similar to the occasional spectacular massive species "die offs" that have occurred on the earth over geological time. Indeed, Dr. Paul C. Light, a professor of public service at New York University predicted at the Great Recession's outset in November 2008 that he expected that 100,000 social profits in the US would vanish from the harsh effects of this current troubled economy.

CNPE's Collaboration Award Concepts

Collaborations are useless unless they can produce mission results. By necessity, then, the advocates and practitioners of collaboration must begin with an absolutely clear understanding of the organization's values and vision. They must be convinced of the key indicators they will rely upon to show evidence that the collaboration is producing the desired outcomes. They must provide themselves a systemic means of collecting and evaluating that data.

Beyond the mission effect, there must be a clear method of measuring the economic benefits that collaboration brings to the effort. This measurement should not be confined to any one agency, but evidenced by how the effectiveness and efficiency of the collaboration brought about wider community benefits in ways that exceed what would have occurred if all the agencies had simply worked alone.

To become an effective collaborating entity, there has to be a culture that educates and rewards active sharing of power and responsibility. People have to be very conscious and deliberate about what advances or retards collaborative behaviors in groups. As natural as it may seem as a group behavior, it demands discipline, understanding and instruction. All levels of the organization—board, staff, and volunteers—should be recruited for their appreciation and regard they give to collaborative behaviors.

※

Section II

ART OF COLLABORATION AWARD WINNERS

Brain Injury Association of Kentucky and Kentucky Family Safety Foundation, 2001

The united efforts of the Brain Injury Association and the Kentucky Family Safety Foundation demonstrated the compelling power of collaboration found in a common goal and proven in a common good.

Recognizing the fact that brain injury is the leading cause of death for children and young adults, and that 90 percent of all brain injuries are preventable, these two organizations teamed up to achieve what neither could have accomplished alone. By pooling their resources and aligning their strategies, they marched toward the common goal of raising public awareness of brain injury and promoting prevention programs that reduce the incidence of brain injury, especially among young people in Kentucky.

They joined forces to educate children about bicycle helmets and provided them at school programs across the state. The Brain Injury Association taught the students about the importance of wearing the helmets. The Kentucky Family Safety Foundation supplied the helmets. Volunteers from both organizations helped fit the students with the proper sizes. Together they instructed and equipped some 1,350 students at 18 elementary schools.

Both agencies worked with television stations in the Louisville and Lexington metro areas to produce TV spots stressing the importance of wearing bicycling helmets.

Furthering their collaborative efforts in this important work, the Brain Injury Association sponsored a women's team in the Race Across

America, a cross-country bicycling competition. The Kentucky Family Safety Foundation contributed $1,000 toward the team's expenses.

Eviction Prevention Advocates Group, 2002
  [Volunteers of America, The Coalition for the Homeless, Housing Authority of Louisville, Legal Aid Society, and Louisville Tenants Association]

In one of the most remarkable and complex interactive collaborations, these five groups found the common cause that united them all and through which they could advance their own aspects of mission.

The Volunteers of America of Kentucky and Tennessee is committed to developing service programs to meet community needs in a fiscally responsible manner, placing priority on programs that promote client self-sufficiency. *The Coalition for the Homeless*' mission advocates for people who are homeless and for the prevention and elimination of homelessness by coordinating the efforts of all agencies in greater Louisville and southern Indiana with similar missions. The *Louisville Tenants Association*'s mission is to improve living conditions, prevent homelessness, increase tenants' rights and responsibilities, and foster better relations between landlords and tenants. The *Legal Aid Society's* mission is to insure that all low-income people have access to justice by providing free legal advice and representation in civil cases. The *Housing Authority of Louisville* provides low-cost housing to persons who are unable to afford such housing in the private market.

The nominated agencies had been meeting since early in 2001 to engage in a dialogue to address the complex issues surrounding the process of eviction of Housing Authority of Louisville tenants. The agencies had to find a common language and understanding of roles in order to address the need to reduce the eviction rate and improve the self-sufficiency of low-income families.

The group worked to find ways to reduce the likelihood of eviction, including:
- researching and disseminating best practices information on reducing evictions

- developing expedient rent reduction procedures
- producing education materials so that tenants are more familiar with their rights and responsibilities
- improving communication among the involved agencies in order to prevent evictions from occurring

As a result of these sustained collaborative efforts, the numbers of eviction filings have fallen significantly. In 2001 the filings fell to the lowest in seven years. The agencies have worked to teach the tenants the needed life skills to help them avert the tragedy of eviction, thereby addressing the problem before it occurs. Over 95 percent of the tenants involved in that education process have remained in stable housing—a remarkable success story of a true collaborative effort.

Louisville Asset Building Coalition, 2003

Center for Women and Families, Coordinating Agency

The Louisville Asset Building Coalition (LABC) is a collaborative effort among a broad group of institutions and community organizations that are working to increase the economic and job stability of low to moderate income working individuals. Established in the fall of 2001, there were over 60 agencies and 120 individuals involved in the work of the Coalition, providing services to families in the areas of tax preparation, financial literacy, asset building, workforce development, and homeownership.

The LABC provides outreach to those receiving the Earned Income Tax Credit (EITC) as well as free tax preparation, access to banking services, financial skills, building courses, and other asset building opportunities.

The goals of the LABC Partnership are to:
- increase the number of qualified individuals who access the EITC
- decrease the amount low-income individuals pay for tax preparation

- connect low-income individuals to financial education, mainstream financial services and asset building initiatives
- create a continuum of economic support services for low income individuals that starts with employment and continues through to asset accumulation and self sufficiency
- identify neighborhood residents who can lead project planning and implementation

The Coalition addressed the tremendous need for better financial services and improved economic literacy programs in Louisville's low- to moderate-income neighborhoods. The gap between access to mainstream financial services and economic support programs can lead to family, financial and employment instability. The Louisville Asset Building Coalition worked to educate people and to provide services under the belief that chances for individual and neighborhood economic success greatly improved when multilevel economic services are made easily accessible and appropriately marketed to all community residents.

The LABC is a powerful coalition made up of for profit, social profit, government and foundation entities that are all committed to the work of asset building for low-income working families. It has demonstrated early success in its ability to work together.

Family and Children First Child Advocacy Center, 2004

The mission of the Family and Children First Child Advocacy Center (CAC) is to strengthen the community by helping families with children maximize their emotional, social, and physical well-being through an array of behavioral health and social services and advocacy efforts.

The Child Advocacy Center displays its collaborative prowess through its involvement in a seamless interaction of law enforcement, forensic, medical care, crisis stabilization, and mental health services all under one roof for victims of child sexual abuse. In the year of this award, it served upward of 1,000 cases of alleged child sexual abuse in and around Jefferson County.

In 2004, CAC was the sole provider of child sexual abuse trauma response services in the Jefferson and Salt River regions of Kentucky. The CAC exists as a collaborative function of law enforcement, physicians, counselors and forensic investigators. It coordinates efforts among multiple police departments, child protective service agencies, mental health agencies, and prosecutors in the Commonwealth Attorney and County Attorney's offices.

The whole point of this collaborative process is to offer comprehensive and unified help to the child. Without this coordinated interactive effort, children are further victimized by the confusion of various bureaucratic processes, turned over to people who are not familiar with the traumatic aspects of the victim being buffeted by well-meaning, but unfocused legal, medical, and social agency functions.

Through this collaborative process, children are spared the agony of repeating their stories endlessly to a series of disconnected authorities. They are given focused, individualized help, and not treated as simple case numbers. Finally, in this joint effort, the coordinating experts are much more likely to piece the puzzle parts together, detect the underlying causes of the abuse, and rescue the child from further mistreatment.

Operation Brightside, Metro Louisville, and Gallapalooza, 2005
(See Spotlight, Section III, p. 81)

Scott County Partnership, 2006

The Scott County Partnership is raising the quality of life in Scott County, Indiana. Its effectiveness comes from its founders' idea that if the people and functioning organizations in the community can unite with common goals they can overcome the problems that they face.

Their vision is to "create a competent, competitive workforce; encourage a robust economy, gainful employment and a high quality of life through initiatives in education, training and social services . . . emphasizing cooperation, performance outcomes and effective use of resources."

The Scott County Partnership was born as an idea in 1995 and as an incorporated entity in 1998. It has fought to improve life in an Indiana county shown to be in the lowest ten percent economic, social and health indicators. Since its work began the Partnership has managed to achieve wonders for the 23,000 residents of Scott County. Among the many advances in the area, during this award year, are the steadily rising education achievement levels and improved median family income levels.

These improvements came about as a result of the collaborative effort of 28 community leaders from business, education, government, and nonprofit organizations forging this Partnership. Their collaboration has been successful in bringing in millions of dollars in grants to help aid programs in education, economic sustainability and self-sufficiency, and youth development. The Scott County Partnership's LifeLong Learning and Workforce Development programs provide workforce training, GED preparation, and a computer lab; the Welfare to Work Task Force provides counseling for victims of substance abuse and high school drop outs, and teen pregnancy prevention; Youth Development and Education programs forge relationships between schools and the community through summer arts programs, after-school programs, and mentoring.

BridgePoint Services & Goodwill of Southern Indiana and Southern Indiana Rehabilitation Hospital, 2007

BridgePoint Services and Goodwill of Southern Indiana empower people with the skills, knowledge, and opportunity to improve their quality of life and to be the best they can be. Just one and a half years prior to this award year, the agency faced having to close a program with a fifty-year history of providing rehabilitative therapies to children with disabilities.

To save this program, BridgePoint Services and Southern Indiana Rehabilitation Hospital (SIRH) entered into a new collaboration. Thanks to this effort, not only was the rehabilitation service for 800 children rescued from extinction, but even more resources were freed up to expand into new programs. SIRH joined forces with BridgePoint and moved into BridgePoint's building, hired BridgePoint's therapy staff, and began offering therapy in the same location.

SIRH is part of a larger network whose partners are Clark and Floyd Memorial Hospitals, Jewish Hospital, and Frazier Rehabilitation Institute. Because of this network, SIRH was able to bring to the collaboration the billing and documentation systems of the larger Jewish Healthcare Network. In one year, because of the efficiency of this larger system, BridgePoint Services was able to recoup a $500,000 loss and new funds became available for new programs focused on autism and at-risk youth.

Both BridgePoint Services and SIRH saw this collaboration as a strategic commitment. They held monthly meetings to insure close collaborative accountabilities were maintained in their joint efforts of grant writing and fundraising. At approximately the same time of this award, this collaboration was also recognized by Goodwill Industries, which honored this successful relationship with the Stewardship Excellence Award.

Phoenix Health Center, St. John Center, and Society of St. Vincent de Paul, 2008

In 2007, Phoenix Health Center, St. John Center, and the Society of St. Vincent de Paul re-ignited their 2004 collaboration to address the barriers faced by chronically homeless individuals. The three organizations received a Department of Housing and Urban Development (HUD) grant to provide permanent supportive housing for chronically homeless individuals with a physical disability, mental illness, and/or chronic substance abuse problem. This project, which began in July 2008, provided permanent housing for 42 individuals at any given time. Using housing vouchers funded by HUD, case managers from Phoenix Health Center and St. John Center moved persons directly from the streets or emergency shelters into apartments throughout the Louisville community. Case managers assisted project participants to obtain housing, disability benefits, employment, and develop skills to maintain their housing. In order to separate the services and housing functions, St. Vincent de Paul served as the fiscal agent for this project and provided housing management services. Twenty-two individuals moved into permanent housing since July 1 of this award year.

Since this collaborations's inception in 2004, these organizations provided housing and supportive services to over 100 chronically homeless men with substance abuse problems. Collaboratively, they have achieved the following outcomes:

- 36 chronically homeless men have obtained permanent housing in the community
- 60 percent of individuals had improved length of sobriety at program exit
- 55 percent of individuals had improved attendance at 12-Step meetings
- 50 percent of individuals had improved contact with a sponsor at exit

The permanent supportive housing project, which began in July 2008, strives to achieve even more lasting outcomes with its partner clients. The Art of Collaboration is often more about achieving better results than it is saving money, although both clearly occur over time. Collaborations such as this one helps all of the organizations address the causes of chronic homelessness better than any one of these organizations could do alone.

Leadership Louisville, 2009

Created in 1979, the Leadership Louisville Center is the region's leading leadership development and civic engagement organization. The Center strives to cross economic and social boundaries to inspire individuals to serve as catalysts for change and a stronger community.

The Make Your Mark Challenge is the service-learning component of Ignite Louisville, the Center's six-month program that prepares the region's emerging leaders to build a better Louisville. Since 2004, Ignite Louisville has collaborated with area social profits to plan, execute, and sustain new strategies for community outreach and success. In return,

Ignite Louisville participants gain experience in community leadership, board involvement, and collaboration.

In 2009, the Make Your Mark Challenge teams worked with eight local nonprofits: Home of the Innocents, House of Ruth, Nativity Academy, Gilda's Club, Dreams with Wings, Exploited Children's Help Organization (ECHO), Cabbage Patch Settlement House, and Family Scholar House (formerly Project Women) to identify needs and create opportunities to contribute to the growth and success of our community's social sector agencies.

Working collaboratively with local social profits, the 2009 class invested about 1200 hours in their Challenge agency, averaging 150 hours per team. Generally, over 50 percent of Ignite Louisville participants continue their involvement with their chosen social profits and 30 percent go on to serve on their boards. Agencies involved in the Challenge report an 83 percent involvement rate for volunteerism and board roles, and almost 70 percent indicate they wouldn't have been successful with their project without the participation of their Ignite Louisville project team. Art of Governance winner, Gilda's Club Louisville, that was also a 2009 Challenge partner says: "Between working with vendors to reduce the price of their services, making gifts themselves, and the man hours given, I would roughly estimate the financial impact to be $50,000."

The collaborative effort between Leadership Louisville and local social profits continues to inspire community involvement that not only leaves a lasting impact on the agencies they serve, but also engages the young professional and emerging leaders to make a positive difference in their community.

Maryhurst and Brooklawn, 2010

Social profits engaging in collaboration often are drawn together because of the close affinity of their mission goals. The first attempt, if successful, builds trust and opens the doors to greater possibilities.

Maryhurst and Brooklawn share similar missions of caring for children who have experienced the trauma of severe abuse and neglect. Both agencies have long histories of providing residential treatment, community-based group homes, and foster care services for children from all across Kentucky. Maryhurt's traditional emphasis has been in residential treatment for severely abused or neglected teenaged girls. Brooklawn, in contrast, is recognized for some of the most successful psychiatric residential treatment services in Kentucky serving young boys.

This year both agencies agreed to launch a joint venture that brings new hope to teenage girls who need intensive therapeutic services. This joint venture, call "MB Care" provides teenage girls with intense psychiatric services in a residential setting, drawing on the strength and successes of both agencies. Maryhurst has a long successful history of serving teenaged girls who have experienced significant trauma from abuse/neglect; Brooklawn has operated some of the most successful psychiatric residential treatment facilities in the state.

The joint program runs as a limited liability entity under a joint board made up of equal representative board members from Maryhurst and Brooklawn and one "at-large" community member who serves as chair. Through the interconnecting of each collaborating agency's strengths, the resulting successes will set the stage for even more, once unimagined possibilities.

Section III

SPOTLIGHT ON: THE ART OF COLLABORATION: BRIGHTSIDE, LOUISVILLE METRO GOVERNMENT, GALLAPALOOZA, 2005

The story of the collaboration of three entities—Brightside, Gallapalooza, and the Metro Louisville government—demonstrates a host of lessons on the dramatic success this behavior can unleash.

Collaboration is a high-wire act. It takes focus, practice, and a tightly integrated balance of intellectual and physical coordination activity to be successful. In its perfect execution, it is a breath-taking wonder to watch. It involves a lot of risk, looks a lot easier than it is, and if anything slips, can result in spectacular failure.

Collaborations can be born of necessity, requiring a great deal of deliberative thought and planning just to bring it to the initiating phase. In other circumstances, opportunities simply present themselves, appearing as suddenly and unexpectedly as Fate knocking at the door. Those opportunistic moments don't simply involve random probability. As the scientist Louis Pasteur reminds us "Chance favors the prepared mind." So does it also show partiality to those organizations that have a collaborative inclination.

This example showcases successful collaboration: Brightside is the Louisville social profit agency that has blended social and public sector efforts in bringing about a clean and green ways of beautifying the Metro Louisville area; this agency worked diligently with a newly created social profit called Gallapolooza and the newly consolidated Metro Louisville government, to achieve new heights of mission accomplishment.

The inspiration came from Brightside's then-board chair, John Conti, CEO of john conti Coffee Company, after his visit to Chicago a few years ago. Intrigued by Chicago's display of large decorated cow "statues" that had been whimsically placed in public locations, he advocated that the same kind of quirky, artistic celebration could grace Louisville streets—but with an obvious difference: using horses instead of cows.

The overall concept proposed to have corporate sponsors put up the funding for the design and production of these life-sized fiberglass horses, and then commission artists to decorate them in their most vivid, imaginative way. Decisions had to be made on where and how to place the horses around the city in prominent public venues during the Derby Festival Week celebrations. After the Derby, the plan envisioned auctioning these artworks with proceeds donated to Brightside to fund its city beautification mission.

Brightside's executive director Cynthia Knapek, noted "We were excited over the whole concept, but the board had very deep concerns over how distracting this would be from our main mission of planting flowers and keeping the city beautified." After further discussions over how to embrace this social entrepreneurial venture, it was decided to create a separate social profit group whose main focus would be to coordinate all these efforts and then pass along the resulting funds to Brightside.

Thus, Gallapalooza was brought into being embracing its main mission to help in the beautification of the city by being a revenue generator for Brightside. Gallapalooza's executive director Lynn Huffman commented, "We were born in to the 'family' as a collaborative partner from the very beginning." She and Cynthia had to form a trusting operational relationship in the fall of 2004 to get this enterprising idea into reality in time for the 2005 Derby.

Both of these social profits' boards had to stay in synchronization with one another as well. There were issues about contacting businesses for sponsorships, selling this never-before-tried venture, and resolving issues all around the production, budgeting, logistics, and ultimate sale of the horses. Fortunately, both boards were graced with a considerable number of well-connected citizens who could "make the phone calls" to others whom they knew would be enthusiastic about bringing this novel concept to life *and* would be willing to help raise funds. The Metro government played its key collaborative role by communicating with the public, talking up the idea, providing regulatory guidelines, and clearance for the safe deployment of these artistic creations.

Cynthia credits Brightside's collaborative culture as being a key ingredient to the success of this endeavor. "When you think about it," she explains, "we have a deep history of forming partnerships with people and agencies in our programs of planting flowers, and similar beautification activities."

This collaboration had several main precarious factors that could have led to crashing failure. Gallapalooza was a brand new agency, just getting its board together, hiring its executive director, and at the same time, embracing a host of responsibilities to complete in a scant six months. The Metro government had only just recently been formed, and there were a great number of issues with which it had to contend—sorting out the merged former city and county departments' roles.

Both Cynthia and Lynn agree that the overall vision of what they were trying to accomplish kept all the participants very focused on what had to be done: some 230 horses, brightly and uniquely painted, placed all over the city to delight the community, and add to the overall excitement of the Derby—in the most novel display of equine splendor in decades.

That first collaborative effort from the newly formed triumvirate of government and two social nonprofits yielded unheralded success. The horses were produced, painted, placed—even lined up in a 'parade' on Fourth Street at one point. Further intensifying their integrated efforts, these three partners reached out to Churchill Downs and to the horse industry in the state to help make people aware and energized about the post-Derby auction. Cynthia admits, "I was very concerned about how much people would be willing to pay for these horses. Since this had never been done before, we had no way of knowing what the level of interest would be as far as purchasing them." As it turned out her fears were quelled when the first auctioned horse went for a winning bid of $8000. Ultimately the total proceeds from all the sales approached $800,000.

Approximately half of this amount went to Brightside; bidders were given an option to designate half of their purchase price to the social profit of their choice. Roughly 150 other social profits were enriched by this massively successful collaboration.

As with many collaborations, this initial success has developed into a continuing successful relationship. Gallapalooza's Lynn Huffman admits, "There was a very real possibility that we would only stay in existence for the first year to pull this whole thing off." But the relationship did continue and is still in effect today. Gallapalooza continues in its mission to help fund Brightside through its artistic programs, but it also plays a role in advising Brightside on the use of the funds. "We don't simply write them a check," Lynn points out, "part of our mission is to advance the beautification of the area, so we have a voice in the effort."

Both of these collaborating directors note that—in modeling their trust and open communication, their clarity of vision in making Louisville a greener and more attractive place to live—all become infected with the spirit of working together. "The true reason we succeed," Cynthia offers," is because everyone sees themselves contributing to a real *community* effort." That goes for the myriad of private sector groups they invite to support them—from banks and trucking companies, to courier services and auto dealers.

The Art of Diversity

CHAPTER 5

"We should all know that diversity makes for a rich tapestry, and we must understand that all the threads of the tapestry are equal in value no matter what their color."
—Maya Angelou

The Center for Nonprofit Excellence once sponsored a national speaker to lead a seminar on the challenges of leadership in governing social profit organizations. Her emphasis at that gathering was the appalling lack of diversity on most of the boards that she had worked with over the years in her consulting business. "Let me summarize this way," she declared, "They are all too male, too pale, and too stale."

In that one lyrical set of adjectives she captured a significant issue upon which the social sector must rivet its attention: diversity. It matters in two significant aspects in this sector's performance. First, diversity matters in the composition of the social profit itself—the people who comprise the organization, whether board, staff, or volunteer force. Second, diversity stands as a key factor in the mission, since it must adapt to the changing demographics of those being served.

Diversity, in its richest sense, means that members of a group possess differences that multiply the group's collective qualities. In our national culture, one must acknowledge, however, that the term "diversity" has an emotional charge to it. It can spark a reflexive synaptic jump. Many people mistakenly link diversity to "politically correct" concepts such as affirmative action and Equal Employment Opportunity rules and regulations. Those are, of course, related to the overall issue of diversity, but do not form the core of the very real sociological depth of this subject.

The United States, in its own historic internal narrative, has acknowledged the strength it has gained from its diversity. America has long described itself as a "melting pot" of cultures and ethnicities, indicating the richness and strength the nation has gained through the absorption and integration of the "many" into one, unique, national, blended identity.

The demographic trends that are evident for this nation in the next forty years point to seismic shifts in the proportional mix of ethnicities. The dramatic rise of the Hispanic segment of our population has led the US Census Bureau to conclude that today's ethnic minorities, now comprising 33 percent of the national population, will rise to 54 percent of the population in America by 2050. What's more, the age shift of the population will have similar social implications: the number of people over age 65 will more than double compared to today's population (38.7 million increasing to 88.5 million).

All of these trends have massive implications regarding the social sector as various organizations form and adapt to the rapidly changing needs driven by this accelerating demographic change. In order to set the stage for these adaptations, it is imperative that the sector pay close attention to the evolving needs now.

Social Profits: Internal Environment

The matter of diversity has nothing to do with political correctness. On-going research in sociology and group dynamics continue to uncover evidence that diversity in groups leads to better decisions, more creative solutions, and better outcomes from their interactions. Over forty years ago, Yale University's research psychologist Irving Janis identified how groups comprised of well-intentioned and very capable people can make disastrously poor decisions as a consequence of what he labeled as "groupthink."

Among the many group characteristics that can lead to calamitous decisions is the lack of social and intellectual diversity. A homogenous group of people sharing the same life experiences, same cultural backgrounds, and same view of the world cannot easily summon up creative opposing points of view. Such groups rarely think "outside the box"; they rarely conceptualize that there even *is* a box.

More recently, James Surowiecki, author of *The Wisdom of Crowds*, noted that the old adage of "two heads are better than one" is potentially true. Groups of people have a higher potential of making better sense of situations and creating enhanced solutions for problems. But the groups have to possess certain characteristics to succeed. Group effectiveness becomes diminished when it lacks "cognitive diversity" in terms of educational, experiential, or occupational knowledge. Diversity brings many more gifts to the table, and opens opportunities to challenge "truths" that an otherwise homogeneous group would never dare question.

Translating these characteristics to boards represents the real work of the social profits.

The first aspect to consider is the board's overall needed skill set to function at all. As a baseline, all board members must be united in their commitment to the mission, values, and vision of the social profit they are entrusted to lead. Here, there is no advantage or allowance for diversity. Beyond that dimension, however, diversity plays a key role, given the board's crucial role in providing overall strategic direction to the organization.

For example, in order to properly function in its fiduciary role, the board needs some form of financial expert on its team, notably an accountant or CPA who can help translate the fiscal data in a manner to help the rest of the board understand. In addition, depending on the social profit's mission, it can be very helpful to have an attorney who can help interpret legal or liability issues; or a medical professional, if the mission has a focus on community health issues; or other relevant expertise.

But diversity must push on beyond the "usual" variants—a board should consider a broader range of categories:

- Geography: Do we have areas of the region we support represented?
- Age: Do we have the richness of outlook represented by the generational views of Baby Boomers (born 1943-1960), Gen Xer's (born 1961-1981), and Millennials (1982-1998)?
- Gender: Does this group have proper representational balance in this most fundamental aspect of our humanity?
- Mission Relevance: Do we have the perspective and voice of those we serve in our presence as board members?
- Influence: Do we have people who have access to the portals of financial or political power to make things happen?
- Time on the Board: Have some of the members served on the board too long? Does the board have a regular influx of new members who can offer fresh inventive perspective, not bound by limits of "we've-always-done-it-that-way" thinking?

As one might imagine, by asking and acting on these questions, the board can break the " too pale, too male, and too stale" syndrome.

One of the toughest challenges in this prescription is the quest to recruit people who "fit" the description and who are willing to serve as a board member. Some will not have had the background, education, or life experiences to believe that they can fulfill a valued role and perspective. Nonetheless, the board needs to foster the growth of these potential candidates for future development into leadership roles.

These same questions can be applied to staff and volunteer resources as well, but with an emphasis on how diversity can translate into day-to-day operational effectiveness in delivering empathetic, compassionate, quality services to those served.

Social Profits: External Environment

One of the abiding questions in the book, *The Five Most Important Questions You Will Ever Ask About Your Organization*, authored by Peter F. Drucker, is: "Who is it we serve?"

The whole point of any social profits' existence is reflected in its mission, but all missions have a targeted group of people who benefit from the mission's focus. That identified group can be as expansive as "victims of armed conflict and other situations of violence" if the organization is the International Red Cross, or can be limited to a few dozen households in a neighborhood alliance. The point is that people being served are not a static population. The underlying demographic changes are making those groups being served more multicultural, more mixed ethnically, and along with those transformations, bringing a significant number of new needs.

For example, at one time in a community, a social profit whose emphasis on serving the poor could work with the presumption that the "face" of the poor could easily be indentified in terms of their specific needs. One could define "poor" in terms of being below a certain income level, as well as other characteristics about housing, family size, etc. In the last generation, however, with rising immigration trends, the influx of refugees accepted in to the community, and other economic trends that have tragically pushed some families into poverty, the social profits have to become more adaptive and inclusive in serving new participants. It now becomes critical that the board act upon the need, for example, that the organization employ multilingual staff and adapt programs that dovetail to the cultural needs of the diverse ethnic groups that have arrived in the community. In fundamental areas such as supplying food to those in poverty, there may be cultural or even biological aspects of what foods would best serve the nutritional needs of that changing community.

CNPE's Diversity Award Concepts

CNPE honors those social profits that have a clear and conscious plan to involve and embrace multicultural and multiethnic participation at all levels of their human resources structure. The board of directors have a rich and diverse set of knowledge, skills, experiences, and a make a conscious effort to promote stakeholders' involvement in guiding the organization toward meeting the needs of the people served. Similarly, the staff and volunteer structures use similar policy guidelines in employing people with the background, skills, cultural heritage, life experiences, and sensitivity that most closely aligns with the served populations' ever-changing needs. All of these attributes ultimately demonstrate more effective strategic decision making and program effectiveness.

In addition, the social profit will have demonstrated a significant adaptability by tailoring its programs to reflect the wider embrace of the changing demographics of the served community. It will consciously plan for and deliver its program services to match the ethnic, age-related, gender, cultural, or geographic trends to insure that its mission success stays in rhythm with the evolving community's changes.

Section II

Art of Diversity Award Winners
Americana Community Center, 2001

(See Spotlight, Section III, p. 101)

Kentuckiana Minority Suppliers Development Council, 2002

Diversity in the social sector often means insuring that the served population has the necessary inclusivity of all segments of a community. The Kentucky Minority Suppliers Development Council won the award in 2002 for its allegiance to this principle.

Through its mission of connecting certified minority business enterprises (MBE's) with corporate America for contracting opportunities, the Kentuckiana Minority Supplier Development Council (KMSDC) has helped racial and ethnic business owners grow their companies through value-added business relationships with corporate and public sector entities in the Kentuckiana region.

KMSDC serves approximately 300 certified minority businesses and over 100 private and public sector corporate members. Of the 300 minority businesses, seventy-five percent are owned by African Americans, nine percent by Hispanic Americans, fourteen percent by Asian/Indian Americans, and two percent by Native Americans.

Through its affiliation with the national council, KMSDC is able to leverage and network support to minority business enterprises so that they can grow their market share beyond the local business community.

Throughout the year, KSMDC sponsors seminars, workshops, and forums designed to help minority businesses strengthen their skills. In addition, this year KMSDC awarded four complete scholarships to members to attend the Executive Management Institutes conducted at Dartmouth University's Tuck School of Business, Northwestern University's Kellogg Scholl of Business Management, and the Minority Business Management Seminar held at the University of Wisconsin. Award winners in this group included one Native American female, two African American males, and one Hispanic American male.

The KSMDC board reflects the rich diversity it advocates as part of its mission, with a mix of twenty-three Hispanic, African American, and Caucasian women and men. KSMDC staff is similarly diverse. In keeping with the spirit of its mission, KSMDC has a policy of purchasing from the minority businesses it supports, this year spending nearly eighty percent of its budget with enterprises owned by minority entrepreneurs.

With KSMDC's advocacy, corporate members spent over $191 million for products and services from minority businesses. In addition, KSMDC member agencies employ over 20,000 people, grossing in excess of $1.35 billion in annual revenues.

Juneteenth Legacy Theatre, 2003

Diversity can be reflected in many different ways—board, staff, participating stakeholders, volunteers, and the served community itself.

Juneteenth Legacy Theatre is a model of diversity in artistic content, board membership, audience participation and community impact. As Kentucky's only professional African American theatre company, Juneteenth Legacy Theatre presents new and original works about the historical and contemporary African American experience. Its audience is sixty-one percent African American and thirty-eight percent white, with nearly sixty percent of audience members describing themselves as new theatre attendees.

Juneteenth is a living model of the value of art for positive change. Director Lorna Littleway has a vision for change through the arts and has a plan to obtain that vision. She works tirelessly to create high quality art and cultivating lasting social change for all who participate in her programs. Guided by Lorna's vision, Juneteenth Legacy Theatre inspires students, community members and other participants to new understandings of challenging social issues by presenting performance art focused on the African American experience.

Juneteenth embraces diversity in its board and staff as well, and includes men and women, African-American and Caucasian board and staff participants, all in an array of ages, occupations and educational backgrounds. As a result, Juneteenth has generated strength through diversity in its governance. Although the majority of its board members are neither practicing artists nor regular theatre-goers, they are interested community members who provide advice and expertise in financial, educational, and partnership matters.

Juneteenth exemplifies extraordinary perseverance and persistence; it demonstrates a rare combination of artistic creativity and iron willed determination to succeed. As a result, it has become a successful organization working for positive social change, offering creative alternatives for a better life in Metro Louisville for all people, regardless of age, race, or ethnicity.

Center for Women and Families, 2004

Diversity not only strengthens an organization, it also gives it the proper tools to work effectively in an ever-increasing diverse nation and community. The Center for Women and Families' experience and reaction to the changing complexion of the community demanded that they take forceful actions to adapt to the need.

The Center exists to serve and advocate on behalf of victims of rape, sexual assault, domestic violence, and families demoralized by economic hardship. The Center serves fourteen counties, seven in Kentucky and seven in Southern Indiana.

In its mission to "meet clients where they are" there's an inherent openness and expectation of embracing diversity. With a reach of over 30,000 constituents in the service area, the clients are diverse in language, culture, age, religion, sexual orientation, economic and employment status, and educational achievement.

The Center has acted in numerous ways to serve these diverse groups. By employing a bi-lingual advocate, the Center provides services to battered immigrant and refugee victims of domestic violence. The Center also recruited "Language Advocates" to serve on behalf of clients in order to facilitate communication and service delivery. This improvement led to other Center decisions in developing staff competence, partnerships and infrastructure—recognized by the Kentucky Domestic Violence Association as a best practice model in the provision of service delivery to diverse clientele.

The Center expanded its outreach to gay, lesbian, bisexual, and transgender (GLBT) victims of violence, through its establishment of a GLBT committee. The Center has actively promoted its presence and availability of help in the GLBT communities.

As a final expression of its commitment to diversity, the Center maintains a diverse governing board and staff, staying conscious of the inherent need and legitimacy these characteristics give the Center in its operational efforts.

Jewish Family & Vocational Service (now known as Jewish Family and Career Services), 2005

Diversity isn't a new concept in this community. Some social profit agencies have been working with successive immigrant populations for over a century. Although the concepts and nature of diversity-related programs may have changed over time, the fundamental principles still apply: be prepared to serve all in need.

Jewish Family & Career Services (JFCS) was established in 1908 to assist immigrants fleeing poverty and persecution, and has clearly carried this commitment to the present. Respect for each individual has led the agency to create innovative programs for the needs of immigrants and refugees from many lands and help them to become active, vital participants in their new communities.

JFCS responds to the needs of immigrants and refugees arriving in our area with services that help them move from poverty and dependence to financial security and self sufficiency. Rooted in the Jewish value of *tikkun olam* ("repair of the world"), the agency's services flow from a respect for each individual and his/her culture.

Years ago, JFCS developed a specialized program in Multicultural Services. Newcomers receive culturally and linguistically appropriate training, counseling, and technical assistance that directly impact their ability to build assets in the form of financial, human and social capital.

JFCS initiated the Immigrant Community Leadership Development program that involves emerging community organizations in planning and service provision. The program recognizes that community leaders of these organizations are best able to identify the needs of their unique communities.

JFCS provides services for older adults and plays a leadership role in a city-wide program that focuses on the needs of elderly refugees. It was at the forefront in developing cross cultural mental health services for Louisville's immigrant community.

In the five years leading up to this award, over 1,200 individuals in 600 families from 37 different countries have participated in Multicultural Service programs. Approximately 450 low income families have developed financial plans that enabled them to save toward purchase of an asset. Over 100 families have purchased homes, 200 individuals have developed career plans.

World Affairs Council of Kentucky and Southern Indiana, 2006

For twenty years, the World Affairs Council (WAC) of Kentucky and Southern Indiana (previously known as the Louisville International Cultural Center) has embodied the spirit of diversity in its ethos and action. Its mission is to enliven a greater cross-cultural understanding in the communities of Kentucky and Southern Indiana. The Council's activities include inviting prominent figures from around the world to speak at their Global Issues and Economic Forums as well as arranging meetings between local organizations and representatives of their foreign counterparts.

The Council brings in 200 to 300 visitors year. These visits not only boost the area's visibility on the globe, but contribute to meaningful and lasting relationships as well. A look at the visitors scheduled in the near future illustrates the high standards of the Council. They include Lech Walesa, former President of Poland, and John Hofmeister, President of Shell Oil.

The Council shows a dedication to diversity through global education. In order to promote cross-cultural education among the area's youth, they have implemented the Academic WorldQuest Competition. This program is a team-based competition on international knowledge. According to the Jefferson County Public Schools Diversity and Multicultural Education Office, WorldQuest has had an impact on students, teaching them to be more globally aware in and out of school. The Council has also organized the Global Education Network—volunteers and institutions work together to provide seminars relevant to current global issues. The most recent events have focused on providing training to teachers in their approach to the Middle East and its complex issues in the classroom.

The World Affairs Council of Kentucky and Southern Indiana is working hard to make the knowledge and culture of the world readily available to the communities in the area, and to make our own way of life known to the world. Their work engenders a strong understanding of global issues and brings people from diverse backgrounds together in openness and exchange of ideas.

Archdiocese of Louisville – Office of Multicultural Ministry, 2007

The Office of Multicultural Ministry (OMM) gives direction, leadership and service to racially diverse groups within the Archdiocese of Louisville and the Metro Louisville community. The agency serves over 12,000 individuals and families in the area and gives direction and leadership to over 40 national offices.

The OMM facilitates cultural inclusion throughout the civic community from an intergenerational perspective. For the last 20 years, OMM has worked to remove barriers new immigrants and refugees face as they learn to live in Metro Louisville. Some of its many services include serving breakfast and lunch; providing computer training, math and reading tutorials; recreation activities that celebrate the cultural arts; physical education; and social studies lessons.

The Catholic Enrichment Center is an extension of the OMM designed to provide cultural enrichment and academic development in addition to outreach ministry. Here, people find answers to many of their questions about how to holistically enhance their lives with a multicultural perspective.

The organization provides opportunities for its staff to fully understand the importance of diversity and creates an environment of appreciation for multicultural customs and ideas. For example, forty-five percent of OMM's workforce is of international origin.

OMM has been a consultant for establishing other offices around the country that wish to do outreach with multicultural populations.

These offices use this agency's programming as a model because of its longevity, the resources OMM provides, and because it is the founding member of a national network of similar offices.

OMM works to ensure that the voices of all people are heard regardless of gender, age, nationality, race, ethnicity or religion by honoring their differences and similarities and working with the Louisville community to support healthy and productive lives for its residents.

Catholic Charities, 2008

Catholic Charities' commitment to diversity speaks through its actions. The agency houses the Kentucky Office for Refugees. Its migration and refugee services department has resettled more than 10,000 displaced persons from thirty countries since its inception in 1975. Catholic Charities' immigration legal services also provide affordable counsel for those seeking to enter the United States on their own.

Settling in a new country that has different societal expectations and norms can be daunting. To assist this transition, Catholic Charities operates an English as a Second Language (ESL) school in partnership with Jefferson County Public Schools. This school serves adults and children, provides childcare, and holds evening classes to accommodate various work schedules. Parenting classes, job skill development and cultural orientation support are also provided.

Too often, cultural differences are not tolerated, much less celebrated. In February and March of 2007, Catholic Charities, the Metro Louisville Office for International Affairs, and the Muhammad Ali Center, sponsored the photographic exhibit, *Surviving Darfur: Staring into the Heart of Human Suffering*. These works helped raise local awareness of the plight of those displaced in that region. Various programs, including media briefings, an educational presentation by the Sudanese representative of Catholic Relief Services, and the screening of the George Clooney film, *A Journey to Darfur*, took place during the month-long event.

In addition to raising awareness that leads to an appreciation of diversity, Catholic Charities offers programs that support and display the boldness to embrace inclusivity. Further, Catholic Charities' staff represents numerous nationalities from five continents who speak over fifteen languages.

Family Health Centers, 2009

As the federal government continues to transform health care services in this country, Family Health Centers (FHC) persist in providing a wide range of programs and services to reduce and eliminate the barriers many persons face when seeking basic health care. While most barriers are financial, FHC increasingly includes language, culture, education, transportation and work schedules.

Last year, over 89 percent of the persons using FHC had incomes below 200 percent of poverty with 74 percent having incomes 100 percent of poverty and below. Black/African Americans comprised 29 percent of all patients; Hispanics/Latinos represented 9 percent. The number of Hispanic/Latino patients increased from 77 in 1989 to 4,002 in 2008, a 5001 percent increase. The number of patients best served in another language increased 112 percent between the years 2005-2008. Limited English Proficient (LEP) patients, speaking 53 unique languages, represented 13 percent of all individual patients in 2008.

FHC recognized LEP patients as an important part of Jefferson County's underserved population and has not only committed to meeting the language needs of its current patient population, but has reached out to immigrant and refugee groups in need of a medical home. In 2007, FHC created the Americana Clinic in South-Central Louisville in order to make high-quality, primary care more accessible to immigrants and refugees, many of whom live in the surrounding area. The Refugee Health Program was established to ensure that comprehensive health screenings, health education, and referral services are provided to Louisville's newly resettled refugees.

As FHC's patient population became more diverse, language was identified as growing barrier to care. Language barriers prevent good communication, increasing the risk of misdiagnosis and medical errors. By training staff to be culturally competent and providing language services to LEP patients, FHC fosters good communication and better patient outcomes.

As a result of FHC's commitment to diversity and communicating across boundaries, over 5,000 individuals were provided with language serves in 2008. In the award year, almost 1,300 refugees received comprehensive screenings and health education in their own language.

Volunteers of America of Kentucky, 2010

One key aspect of diversity in the social sector is the ability to mirror the community's needs by employing people who reflect the culture, values, and "face" of that those whom it serves. This fosters trust and understanding, and contributes to successful outreach to communities that might not otherwise be involved.

The Volunteers of America of Kentucky's mission is to create positive changes in the lives of individuals and communities it serves. One of its programs entitled "Stop the Transmission of HIV/AIDS Outreach Program (STOP) fights the perception that HIV/AIDS is no longer a public health threat and targets high-risk populations for educational and testing services. In this way, the STOP program hopes to prevent and/or reduce the spread of HIV/AIDS. The STOP prevention specialists travel to places that are generally unreached by the public health system: adult bookstores and other public sex environments to establish a network of contacts where the information is needed most.

From a diversity standpoint, the VOA's 758 full and part-time employees largely mirror the population they serve. Sixty-one percent of its employees are African-American and 36 percent are white. In 2009, 49 percent of the clients served were African-American and 48 percent were white. In addition, the Hispanic proportion of VOA is 1.2 percent, reflecting closely the community's 1.3 percent Hispanic presence. But there's even a deeper diversity reflection. Diversity also means interacting in a trusting environment between caregiver and recipient. This means that VOA's work includes outreach to "pride" organizations and activities, establishing a valued and trusted role in spreading the STOP program's message in the fight against HIV/AIDS.

Recognizing the spread of HIV/AIDS now accelerating in the Hispanic/Latino community, VOA has hired a Spanish-speaking prevention specialist to create an improved outreach to that community and build the bridge to offer education and prevention. Diversity has become a key strategic facet of VOA's programmatic efforts to assist those who are at risk or currently suffer from HIV/AIDS. By embracing this approach they have set the stage for dramatically improved mission success.

Section III

**SPOTLIGHT ON: ART OF DIVERSITY:
AMERICANA COMMUNITY CENTER, 2001**

It would be difficult if not outright impossible to find another social profit in the region that could come anywhere close to matching the diversity work that represents the very heart and soul of Americana Community Center (ACC).

At almost every waking hour of the day, the ACC is a beehive of endless program activity, providing services to children and adults living in Louisville from these nations: Afghanistan, Albania, Algeria, Argentina, Benin, Belize, Bosnia, Bulgaria, Burma, Burundi, Cambodia, Chile, China, Columbia, Congo, Croatia, Cuba, Dominican Republic, Ecuador, Egypt, El Salvador, Ethiopia, Gambia, Guatemala, Guinea, Haiti, Honduras, Hungary, India, Iraq, Ivory Coast, Japan, Jordan, Kenya, Kosovo, Laos, Liberia, Libya, Mexico, Morocco, Nepal, Pakistan, Panama, Paraguay, Peru, Poland, Puerto Rico, Russia, Rwanda, Senegal, Serbia, Sierra Leone, Somalia, South Korea, Sudan, Tanzania, Thailand, Togo, United States, Uruguay, Uzbekistan, Venezuela, Vietnam, and Yemen.

The ACC's mission is to provide a spectrum of services for the many diverse residents of Metro Louisville. These services enable people to discover and utilize resources to build strong families, create a safe, supportive community and realize their individual potential.

The Americana Community Center emphasizes diversity as a cornerstone value in all levels: governance, programs and services. The vibrant mix of refugee families and American families present both unique challenges and opportunities for the work conducted by the center.

The Americana Community Center offers programs that:
- encourage the sharing of cultures and customs
- provide skills to break down racial and ethnic tension
- create opportunities to build trust and self-esteem
- support the development of supportive family relationships and teamwork

Beyond that, the Americana Community Center advocates the inclusion of its members through educating the wider community on the value of diversity within society.

Examples of their key work range from conducting youth programs, family education sessions, and adult education classes; teaching children how to get along with children from other cultures; to acculturating people to the US customs and values; providing educational guidance and structure in the after-school tutoring programs; and hosting a Family Health Center site on their campus.

Diversity's advantages grace their staff and board as well. A range of ethnic, gender, and national origin diversity provide evidence of Americana's commitment to more fully understanding the needs of Louisville's growing immigrant community.

Edgardo Mansilla, the long-term executive director and a native of Argentina, explains, "People who have experienced coming to this country without knowing the language or customs are much more aware and sensitive to these needs. They can recall the feelings of fear and uncertainty that occur when coming to a new land."

Pointing out that Louisville has somewhere between 85,000-100,000 immigrants representing 12-13 percent of its population, Edgardo sees this as both a challenge in supporting the successful integration of internationals, as well as a gift to our community. "We strongly believe in the multicultural values of a society," he emphasizes.

It isn't just a matter of getting people to adapt to American values and culture. It's equally important that this rich mix of people understand, share, and interconnect with one another. Edgardo looks to the large Family Garden plot that is overflowing with emergent produce. "We see people from different lands, planting different kinds of food, talking to one another and their children about vegetables they perhaps have never seen before, and the different ways to nurture the crops to harvest," he explains. The cross connection of ideas, experience, and knowledge fosters better understanding and creativity.

Another testimony to their community-wide breadth and inclusion is reflected in their list of partners. ACC maintains relationships between agencies that help with ACC's mission work, working in partnership with the Jefferson County School System, a number of universities and colleges around the state, and other cultural support groups such as the Burundi Community of Kentucky, the Latino-Hispanic coalition, and Somali Association of Louisville.

Despite the dramatic growth that ACC has enjoyed from its original 2,500 square-foot space to its current 50,000 square-foot facility on the campus of the former Holy Rosary High School in south Louisville, the need and demand for services in this region relentlessly challenge ACC. "Every program we conduct has a long waiting list of families and children who need to participate in our activities," Edgardo points out. It is clear that ACC will continue to meet that growing demand.

The Next Decade:
New Areas of Excellence

CHAPTER 6

"As for the future, your task is not to foresee it, but to enable it."
—**Antoine de Saint-Exupery**

The Center for Nonprofit Excellence remains committed to its mission of serving as a catalytic agent in its quest to develop the social sector's capacity to succeed in this region. In a recent strategic planning session, CNPE's board revised the Center's mission to proclaim the CNPE is charged with "co-creating a vibrant, exemplary nonprofit community in Greater Louisville through collaboration, shared learning, advocacy, and the promotion of innovation and excellence." This revison contains significant changes from the original mission. That earlier edition promised to support the sector "through offering information, helping nonprofits realize their mission and achieve excellence."

The Center will now expand its role from a primary repository and dispenser of social sector knowledge to a much more extensive role, one that:

- fosters interactions and encourages the sharing of ideas
- convenes social sector participants in forums to share and create new learning
- seeks and promulgates best practices

- promotes adaptive change
- encourages building a community of collabrative, learning organziations

This change will also herald consideration of new areas of excellence that must be promoted. Aside from the traditional five areas of Vision, Governance, Leadership, Collaboration, and Diversity, in this next decade CNPE will create two new areas that reflect the growing social sector need in this community.

The Art of Innovation

The nineteenth century English biologist Thomas Huxley claimed, "It is the customary fate of new truths, to begin as heresies, and to end as superstitions." In order to survive in this coming decade, the social sector will have to produce a few good heretics.

The current economic downturn, now approaching its second year with no clear path to recovery in sight, will continue to strain the social sector in enormous ways. Traditional funding sources will be more constricted in their ability to provide resources. Demands for social sector services will grow at progressive rates. Caught in the crushing tension of these opposing forces, many social profits will not survive unless they emulate the unofficial mantra of the US Marine Corps: "adapt, improvise, and overwhelm." The social profits that will survive this crisis will have to: (1) create new pathways of streamlining their operational effectiveness; (2) re-invent sustainability models; and (3) form intercommunity relationships in ways that defy traditional standards and logic.

The Center will be true to its revised mission by identifying and evangelizing those revolutionary ideas under this award category.

The Art of Generating New Leadership

The Center has always regarded leadership as a key factor in social profit success, but the emphasis has been on people in current leadership positions. Three years ago a national survey of social sector executive directors showed that 75 percent planned to retire from that position within this next decade. Although most of those individuals indicated that they're willing to stay involved in the social sector, it is clear (since many are approaching retirement age) that they are yearning to be relieved of the pressures of formal leadership. Who, then, will succeed them? Are there individuals ready to accept the enormity and complexity of the issues in the coming decade? The same survey data indicated that only 50 percent of those current leaders were preparing their potential successors. Are those who are being readied for command being taught the old "superstitions" or are they being nurtured to be the new heretics/innovators?

The same challenges apply to board leadership. Although board chairs do not have the same average tenure as an executive director in the social sector, that board leadership role plays a pivotal part in the board's ability to govern well. To the extent that a board carefully grooms this key leader position, that too, will be a consideration under this award category.

With these additions and the continued emphasis on the historic five original Arts, CNPE hopes to enhance the sector's vitality and refresh—in all social profits—the faith, devotion, and capacity to build a better world.

ABOUT THE AUTHOR

Eric Schmall joined Louisville's Center for Nonprofit Excellence (CNPE) as Director of Consultation in 2001. Five years later, Eric earned his designation as a licensed consultant with the Standards for Excellence® Institute, a national initiative that promotes the highest standards of ethics and accountability in the social sector.

Since joining CNPE, Eric has successfully designed and facilitated over 700 classes, retreats, workshops, and seminars on leadership, teamwork, board governance, project and systems management, board development, and strategic planning cycles for hundreds of social profit organizations in the Kentucky and Southern Indiana region.

Eric has been in consulting and management for nearly forty years. For most of that era he worked in the private sector in various capacities as a research analyst, manager, and consultant. He is a native of Louisville, Kentucky and has spent most of his career in that community.

Eric can be contacted at CNPE directly at (502) 618-5329 or via email at eschmall@cnpe.org.

ABOUT THE CENTER FOR NONPROFIT EXCELLENCE (CNPE)

CNPE embraces a mission of co-creating a vibrant, exemplary social sector community in Greater Louisville through collaboration, shared learning, advocacy, and the promotion of innovation and excellence.

Founded in 1999, the Center for Nonprofit Excellence is a 501(c)(3) social profit management support organization that provides a central point to access information about the social profit sector, promulgates best practices, instructs in the realm of board and staff professional enrichment, and offers individualized consultation—all to advance the social sector's quest to maximize the Louisville, Kentucky region's greater good.

Serving over 350 regional social profit members who subscribe to its services, CNPE also enjoys the membership support of twenty area foundations, forty-one individuals, and forty-one corporate sponsors.

CNPE's office is located in downtown Louisville in the Brown Theatre Building @ArtSpace. Its mailing address is 323 West Broadway, Suite 501, Louisville, KY 40202. CNPE's office can be reached by phone at (502) 315-2673, by fax at (502) 315-2677, or by visiting its website at www.cnpe.org.

CNPE's Chief Executive Officer, Kevin Connelly, can be contacted directly at (502) 618-5331 or via email at kconnelly@cnpe.org.

CENTER FOR NONPROFIT EXCELLENCE
Your Excellence Is Our Passion

CENTER FOR NONPROFIT EXCELLENCE

REFERENCES

Collins, J. (2005). *Good to Great in the Social Sectors.* New York: Harper Collins.

Drucker, P. (2008). *The Five Most Important Questions You Will Ever Ask About Your Organization.* San Francisco: Jossey-Bass.

Greenleaf, R.(1998). *Servant Leadership.* New York: Paulist Press.

Janis, I. (1983). *Groupthink.* New York: Houghton-Mifflin.

Kouzes J. Posner, B. (2007). *The Leadership Challenge.* San Francisco: Jossey-Bass.

Reina, D. Reina, M. (1999). *Trust & Betrayal in the Workplace.* San Francisco: Berrett-Koehler Publishers.

Sinek, S. (2009). *Start With Why.* New York: Portfolio.

Surowiecki, J.(2005). *The Wisdom of Crowds.* New York: Anchor Books.

Suzuki, S. (2006). *Zen Mind, Beginner's Mind.* Boston: Shambhala Publications.

If we know where we are and something about how we got here, we might see where we are traveling—and if the outcomes which lie naturally in our course are unacceptable to make timely change.
—ABRAHAM LINCOLN

PRAISE FOR CNPE

It was a pleasure being part of this strategic planning experience. Mr. Schmall's facilitation was excellent—energetic and enlightening. I appreciate all that you and the board do for Day Spring. I felt the time this weekend was well spent. I am committed to the continuing process of our planning.

—*Gail Rooney, MSSW*
DAY SPRING, LOUISVILLE, KY

I count on CNPE to understand the realities of running a nonprofit business and offer training and other opportunities to meet those needs. The 4-C staff and I have attended sessions on everything from Development of an IT plan to Social Entrepreneurship.

—*Susan A. Vessels, Executive Director*
COMMUNITY COORDINATED CHILD CARE (4-C),
LOUISVILLE, KY

I believe I speak for the group when I say that last night's meeting was a great success. I thought you really exceeded the expectations. Your expertise and insight we're clearly what made the process work. You engaged the group in ways that gave everyone a sense of importance, ownership and enthusiasm. Clearly, everyone was also much more informed. The value of these meetings a couple of times a year was really underscored by the whole experience.

—Annie Rosenberg-Sattich, President
Zoom Group, Louisville, KY

I, along with the Louisville Urban League, have experienced real value from the work of the Center for Nonprofit Excellence. From their work in leadership development, board work, emerging executives, and their annual conferences, they bring to the table a number of offerings that help enrich our social and arts sectors. We applaud their commitment to quality, inclusivity and the importance of the nonprofit sector. I especially applaud the leadership of Kevin Connelly who has tenaciously championed the work CNPE and made it a worthy partner and collaborator. Congratulations!

—Benjamin K. Richmond, President & CEO
Louisville Urban League, Louisville, KY

The Center for Nonprofit Excellence helps further the value and valor of the many people who support and work in the nonprofit sector. The Metro United Way is proud to have helped launch the work this fine organization does both with and for our community. We are excited by the publication of *Striving for Excellence in the Social Sector: A Decade of Distinction* because we share the belief that a good way to build excellence into the way civic work is accomplished is to recognize and celebrate it.

—Joe Tolan, President & CEO
Metro United Way, Louisville, KY

Throughout these opportunities for me as a nonprofit leader and Family Scholar House as a young but growing nonprofit organization, CNPE has offered information, guidance, collaboration, problem-solving tips and access to your highly qualified staff. I often refer others to CNPE and encourage all new nonprofit leaders to join as this is one of the best investments we have made.

For many of us, CNPE is so much a part of our nonprofit community that we forget how fortunate we are to have this collaborative organization in our community as a vital resource. Not only do nonprofit organizations benefit, but our community at large also benefits from the leadership that you and your staff bring to the business of supporting the organizations that support our community.

—Cathe Dykstra, President & CEO
FAMILY SCHOLAR HOUSE, LOUISVILLE, KY